MARVELLOUS

isn't it?

Also by Ron Manager

Stuffed – the exciting account of Ron Manager's futile attempts to stuff dead animals and pass it off as taxidermy

Slalom: My Uphill Struggle in the Men's Downhill – the exciting account of Ron Manager's futile attempts at Olympic Glory

Shalom – the exciting account of Ron Manager's futile attempts to ingratiate himself with the Jewish community of North London

MARVELLOUS
isn't it?

THE AUTOBIOGRAPHY

RON MANAGER

headline

First published in 2002 by
HEADLINE BOOK PUBLISHING

10 9 8 7 6 5 4 3 2 1

Cataloguing in Publication Data is available from the British Library

ISBN 0 7553 1076 4

Typeset in Sabon by Palimpsest Book Production Limited
Polmont, Stirlingshire

Designed by Ben Cracknell

Printed and bound in Great Britain by
Clays Ltd, St Ives plc

Headline Book Publishing
A division of Hodder Headline
338 Euston Road
London NW1 3BH

www.headline.co.uk
www.hodderheadline.com

To my wife Joan for her tireless work editing my words, and also –

Frank Tuft
Wally Cusp
Eddie Cleak
Ken Bates
Sol Pardew
Mickey Nip

– Gone, but not forgotten!

Ron, they're not all gone yet.

Well, just cross out the ones that haven't gone then.

I can't do that, Ron.

Yes you can, it'll only take a minute.

Why don't you do it then?

Are you helping or not?

Contents

FOREWORD

ROCK BOTTOM

Here comes Manager! He's clean through on goal with only the keeper to beat again. Yess! It's two–nil and the young Ron Manager is showing the Italians how to play the game, and let's remember they are the world champions. He's really on fire here today and the meanest defence in the world simply can't handle him. He's picked up the ball on the left now, and he's passed one man, two, it's extraordinary the ball seems to be glued to his feet. My word he's going to make it three, surely it's a hat-trick for Ron Manager . . .

'Come along, sir. Wakey, wakey! Has sir been at the bottle again?'

AND that was how yours truly, Ron Manager, woke up on Friday 20th March, 1992, my playing career a distant memory, my marriage to the long-suffering Joan on the rocks, my managerial career in tatters, my undergarments in shreds. The occasion? The morning after an undignified third-round exit from the Cup at the hands of lowly Fortnum & Mason FC of the Argos Conference. The location? Underneath a park bench – my bed for the night. The reason? My 'alcohol problem'. Though I didn't see it as such. Oh no, I was Charlie Big Potatoes. The previous evening I had consumed an incredible three pints of best bitter and two glasses of wine. Not just any old wine – red wine! Astonishingly I was still alive to tell the tale. Not that I was coherent enough for anyone to understand it. Certainly not the poor policeman who'd woken me from my drunken reverie. How he could have known that the shambling soiled wretch slumped before him, reeking of God knows what – well, horseshite actually – was none other than Ronald Ivanhoe Manager?

'Where do you live, sir?' I struggled to make sense of the question. 'Live? . . . Hmm . . . isn't it? . . . Ho ho! Wasn't it? . . . Marvellous!'

I'll never forget the look on his face as the realisation slowly dawned. 'F**k me, it's Ron Manager!' And fuck me, he was right.

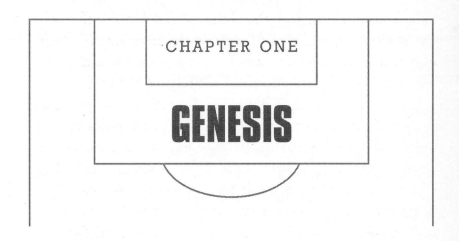

CHAPTER ONE

GENESIS

'Oooh, Mrs Manager . . . It's a boy!'

'Yes, he's lovely, isn't he? I'm going to call him Ron.'

HO HO, only joking! If you're just settling down, expecting to enjoy a sentimental trawl through my lachrymose childhood memoirs, best to bugger off back to the bookshop and see if they'll let you exchange this for something by one of those actor Johnnies – tell 'em Ron sent you!

Let's bang on with the football! Hold tight for an edge-of-seat, roller-coaster ride through the giddy hurly-burly world of football – the tears and tantrums, the teacups and, er, tofu of football's inner sanctum. Hold on to your hats, it's going to be a white-knuckle ride!

But first you probably want to read a bit about me – Ron Manager! I eat, sleep, breathe and wear football! I drive it! I've scaled the dizzy heights and plumbed the murky depths – ha ha! – not much! So here we go . . .

Ron's Most Memorable Moment? Well it's the same as everyone else's, isn't it? Torville and Dean – Bolero, wasn't it? – still causes a strange stirring in the loins, hmm? No, hang on a minute, maybe Erica Roe, ho ho Twickers – marvellous! It's a toss-up between the two, isn't it, hmm?

Here, bet you can't guess this one! Ron's Favourite Colour? Ho ho! I always get asked this one. In fact it's a kind of turquoise – maybe aquamarine is the closest you get – I've even had the bathroom done in it.

Ron's All-Time Hero? To be serious for a second, it's got to be Davy Crockett, 'wrastling' bears in the Florida Everglades. He had three ears, you know – a left ear, a right ear, and another one that, er, escapes me at the moment. Some fellow, hmm? You won't see his like again! Marvellous!

Er, oh yes, football, hmm? The wild frontier, isn't it? And Ron Manager has travelled each and every highway – and byway – you tak' the high road an' ah'll tak' the low road – we all have our ups and downs. Ah!

Ron's Ups? Ho ho, we'll get to those later on!

Ron's Downs? Er, 11th June, 1958, hmm? Some blight**'s had the tail off my Davy Crockett hat – I was gutted!

Ron's Regrets? Hmm? I've had a few, but then again, er, no time to go into them all here. Where was I? Oh yes, I've travelled each and every highway. Regrets? I've had a few . . . Actually I have had a few tonight, er . . .

Can we start this again in the morning? Joan? You haven't gone to bed have you?

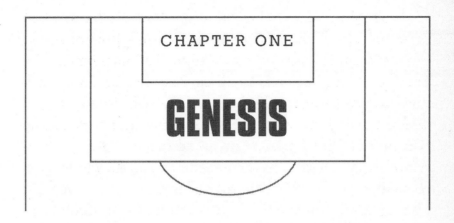

CHAPTER ONE

GENESIS

'Hey missus, can we have our ball back?'

Phufff . . . sssssss . . .

THE saddest sound in the world, isn't it, hmm? My earliest memories are of listening to the passionate cries of young boys enjoying an innocent kickabout, as my Auntie Dolly pushed me round the park – I can't have been long out of my perambulator at the time.

'Deadly Dolly' they called her – her hat-pin always at the ready. Marvellous!

Jumpers for goalposts! Isn't it? Those endless summer days, kicking through the piles of frosty autumn leaves – often a little dog-muck in the leaves – sometimes a dead body found by dog-walkers. I often wonder how many poor souls would ever be found without their help? We might now look on them as pariahs of society, standing proudly by as their slobbering hounds foul our public spaces, but would we rather have our parks full of rotting cadavers? Let's salute the dog-walkers! Marvellous!

Right ho, let's bang on. I was born in 1932 into a little-known mining community in north-east London called Ponders Bar. Don't go looking for it, it's no longer there. Where has it gone? I have absolutely no idea. And to let the truth be known, I don't really care.

I've always been a wanderer, mentally, physically and romantically. Don't tell the wife – ha ha! – but I've certainly been around a bit during the all too brief time allotted to me here on this earth. Oh yes, isn't it? I've travelled a long way down the road from my humble beginnings as the seventh son of a London miner.

In those far-off days the signs of the Depression were all around us and the Second World War and the menace of Hitler's Germany loomed over us, and I do mean loomed. As the youngest of three boys it was rare that there wasn't something looming over me – often in the shape of a demented sibling wielding a shovel, or maybe a purloined axe. In that respect we were like any other family growing up in a tight-knit community – educated at the school of hard knocks.

Looking back, I suppose I was always a bit of a loner, a bit of a dreamer – bit of a tosser, actually – but I soon realised I had inherited a strange innate affinity with the old air-filled pig's bladder. And I had one glued to my feet from birth – literally! So it was some years later that I realised I was a bit of a dab hand with a football as well. Be fair, even Stanley Matthews couldn't have demonstrated his silky skills on the ball with something stuck to his foot. Even Pelé in his pomp wouldn't have tried to chip the goalie from the half-way line with a bloomin' pig's bladder bobbling about on his toe. But this was before his time. Innocent days!

Who was the defining influence on my future career, hmm?

In a word, Stanley. In his pomp, he was everything I wished to be – bustling, indefatigable, confident. Swaggering around with that low centre of gravity. Marvellous!

A confused, bewildered, under-achieving adolescent, I was still finding my feet, literally. I knew something was afoot when I was left home alone one evening with Stanley. Stan was in a somewhat playful and peckish mood – quite out of character for a dachshund! And if it's fair to say that my life changed overnight, then so did Stanley's. He never had that confident swagger afterwards – an air-filled pig's bladder makes a terrible pop when you get a bit of purchase on it with your canines.

And so, at last unencumbered, I was free to dedicate myself to the beautiful game and escape the underground tyranny of the coalface.

What is it about mining communities and football? Think of the greats – Matt Busby, Bill Shankly, Bob Paisley, Alan Ball – pretty much all from good mining stock. But I so nearly didn't go down the soccer road. Father had other plans for yours truly – well, me actually – he may have had plans for yourself, had he known you, but Ron Manager deals in hard facts, not idle speculation.

Dad was a typical miner, hard as nails with a soft underbelly. Not that anyone saw his underbelly unless he'd had a few. And then out it would come, that great soft under-belly looming out from under his overbelly, as he regaled us all with a few choruses of 'The Old Bamboo' in his resonant, reedy, high tenor. Then, when suitably maudlin, it would be a sentimental song and a clip round the ear before bedtime. Marvellous!

From an early age it had been assumed that I would follow my father and my two brothers, Tom and Eddie, down the pit. A couple of rough diamonds, Tom and Eddie loved the subterranean life and the brutish cama-raderie of the coalface. They were also accomplished boxers, often combining boxing and mining to great effect. The sight of them as they emerged, blinking into the sunlight after their shift, with coal-blackened faces and tremendous cauliflower ears, filled our old dad with fatherly pride fit to burst, literally. As far as he was con-cerned, boxing was king, football was for pansies. But then, my father was born with two left feet. No really, he was! But he turned it to his advantage. Though it might have put him off the beautiful game, it certainly saved him a fortune swiping shoes from the bargain bins out-side Mr Byrites.

Well, my father might not have been a well-educated man but luckily I inherited my mother's keen intellect. She was the thinker of the family. 'Ron,' she used to tell me, 'your dad's as thick as arseholes. Life's short and point-less so get on with it, son.' Marvellous!

And so I found myself headed for Craven Cottage, hoping to take my first tentative steps into the heady, giddy, ultimately meaningless world of professional

sport. A little reticent, a little hesitant – a little boy –
yet bouyed . . . Is that how you spell it? It is, isn't it?
Well if it isn't, Mrs Manager can sort it out, that's what
she's paid for. Me and Joan have always been self-
sufficient, so why pay for a proofreader when you can
keep it in-house?

What do you reckon, Joan?

Blinding, Ron.

Yes, buoyed with my mother's homespun wisdom, I set
off for Craven Cottage with a spring in my step. However,
my joy was short-lived. Just as I thought I'd got my foot
in the boot-room door I found it kicked shut by the jack-
boot of Nazi Germany.

Yes, a little something called World War Two had
started. What a kick in the wotsits, Adolf! – mind you I
was only seven at the time.

Joan, how many words is that so far? Oh, is that all? Right ho, I'll
bang on a bit then.

Well, father might have been a little old-fashioned even for
those days, not a literary man – bet he never thought his
youngest son would one day be writing a book! Even the
thought of reading one would have sent him to bed with
brain-fever – but he certainly shaped my thoughts, and the
words of wisdom passed down from his own father and
his father's father and his mother's father's father (my

father's father's father's mother never being entirely sure who my father's father's father's father actually was – though we all have our suspicions. Great-great aunt Nellie reckoned he was the queen's physician – the jury's still out on that one, ho ho!) Er, sorry . . . Where was I? Er, speak as you find, isn't it?

And though most people thought of my father as nothing more than an uneducated, pugnacious, semi-literate bigot, it was him what made me the man I am today – and I'll batter anyone what says otherwise! Ho ho, that's one of my 'funnies'. Don't worry, you'll get used to them.

But whatever people say about my father, his paternal advice still rings as true today*, as it did back then**, 'Walk tall, walk straight and look the world right in the eye.'

Many's the night he'd return from his club to find me curled up on the armchair with the latest Enid Blyton. And though dishevelled, bleary and boss-eyed with drink, his paternal instincts would come to the fore, and he'd slur the words of wisdom that had been passed down from his, . . . er, you know, all that lot I told you about earlier.

'Son, stand up and be counted!'

I respected him for it – despite knowing that at the count of 'two', he would steal the vacant armchair and I would be condemned to another night in the communal bed with Tom, Eddie and a few of the regulars he'd brought back

---

★ Thursday.
★★ Yesteryear.

from the Anchor and Hope. What the heck! He taught me to take responsibility for my actions.

So what attracted me to the beautiful game and a life of football? Blame my Uncle Bert.

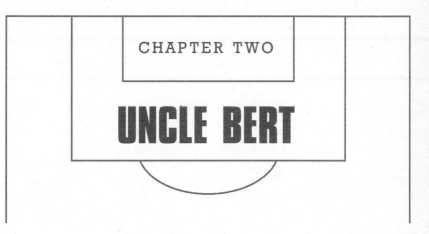

CHAPTER TWO

UNCLE BERT

'Oi Ref! Where's your specs?'

LET he amongst us who hasn't bawled himself hoarse with that one, cast the first meat pie, hmm? Marvellous, isn't it?

That was my Uncle Bert coaching his works' team, in the old Southern Isthmian League⋆ (before the money-men got involved and renamed it the Argos Catalogue⋆⋆).

And that was my introduction to the passionate world of football.

'. . . when all around are doing their pieces . . .' Bert would be doing his pieces with the 'wanker in the black' big-time!

⋆ Isthmian, relating to or situated in the Isthmus of Corinth or Panama.
⋆⋆ Christmas, 1989.

But, be fair, having to make a spur-of-the-moment decision in the blood and thunder of a Cup tie – it's the hardest job in football, isn't it? And we've all got our own interpretation of the rules.

But that's where my obsession with the beautiful game began. And it is beautiful, isn't it? hmm?

A bag of chips and a thick ear on the way home – marvellous! And as we trudged wearily through the streets, Bert would tell me the laws of football, until I could recite every one of them off by heart. Even if some of the language had me frankly baffled, the sheer poetry of them rolling off his tongue held me utterly spellbound. And once committed to memory, it never leaves you. Here's one from the handbook . . .

'Law 11: If a player deliberately trips an opponent who is standing in an offside position, in the penalty area, who doesn't attempt to play the ball or obstruct, a penalty kick should be awarded.'

Ho ho! Great stuff, hmm? Marvellous! Hats off to my Uncle Bert! I was never actually sure which side of the family he was from, but he was certainly my mother's favourite. You couldn't help but notice how she always fluttered her eyes at him, in a way that I would latterly come to recognise as 'coquettish'. With father working his guts off, I came to look on Bert as my father figure, and my mother did nothing to discourage me.

He took me under his wing, and rescued me from a life of juvenile delinquency – teddy boys, drape coats, brothel creepers and razor gangs. And despite still harbouring a dark brooding resentment for the bl***ter who'd had the tail off my Davy Crockett hat, he kept me on the straight and narrow. As opposed to the, er, bendy and thick, I suppose, hmm?

Quite a character, my Uncle Bert. He'd been quite a handy player himself in his day, and had spent some time on the books with Grimsby. Not your typical frustrated journeyman, as a striker all that was missing from his game was a few goals. Ask your granddad if he remembers Bert Hitchcock. You'll probably have to jog the dotty old bugger's memory. Try telling him Bert 'Psycho' Hitchcock. If that doesn't work just tell him Fulham '41 – or something – I can't ever remember who he played for myself.

As for that nickname – 'Psycho', hmm? Curious, I always thought – you couldn't have met a more laconic, mild-mannered kind of fellow. And it was only years later I discovered it was because he'd stuffed his first wife and kept her in a rocking chair in the west wing. Yes, really.

When the police finally hauled him off many years later – my uncle shouting and screaming and lashing out furiously – even as I listened to my mother telling the neighbours he'd been 'stitched up good and proper' – I couldn't help but think, that if only Auntie Jessie had been afforded a similar degree of craftsmanship, I wouldn't have gone home covered in sawdust each night after giving her a parting hug. Marvellous!

But Bert it was who took me to my first ever football game. Derby against Charlton in the FA Cup final, 1946. Not that I remember much about it. After all, I was only a mere teenager at the time. But the memories I do have will stay with me to my dying day . . . Er . . . the ball burst . . . and er . . . enjoying a wee on the twin towers with my Uncle Bert on the way home. And he confided in me that he'd always dreamed of winning an FA Cup medal for his father, 'Wild' Bill Hitchcock, a typical frustrated journeyman who'd had trials for Grimsby in the twenties.

From that day on I was obsessed with football*. While the rest of the old gang were hanging out at the youth club, chatting up the girls from the local convent school, and dancing furiously to George Formby, I was out under the lamppost – not the one George was leaning on! – ho ho, I've got my witty hat on! (Don't worry, you'll get used to it. I've got a couple more 'funnies' I'll try and bung in before the end.)

Er, yes . . . While the rest of the old gang were 'getting their ends away'**, I was either helping out at the local donkey sanctuary or I was dribbling round a lamppost, hoofing a ball about in the cobbled streets around my home, and developing all the skills which would sustain me through my long and tedious career. As I darted under the streetlight I was no longer in Burnt End, I was striding Turf Moor or Ayresome Park, depending on which alleyway I'd punted it into that night. One evening I unleashed an unstoppable volley on my wrong foot which cannoned off a passer-by and disappeared over a wall. Climbing to

---

* Tuesday. Sorry, I put the asterisks in the wrong place. If you looked this up to find out what football is, you must be a right *rse.
** They bloomin' weren't, the lying bl**mers.

retrieve it – Blow me! – there was Uncle Bert and my mother in a heap on the ground. I must have hit the ball with such venom I'd knocked them clean off their feet and partially removed their clothing.

You wouldn't believe it to see me now, but I was a shy and solitary youth, comfortable only in my own company. But then one night I was suddenly aware of a hulking figure lurking in the shadows behind the dustbins, which in my boundlessly fertile imagination were Wembley's twin towers. It was Norman, the son of the local butcher. Although I'd seen him around, as a shy youth I'd never spoken to him. But this time I screwed my courage to the sticking point.

'Do you want to join in?'

'I'm havin' a pee, mate!'

Ron Manager had made a friend! From then on me and Big Norm were inseparable, literally. Two young lads striving to make our names in the world of football. Was this chance or destiny? Uncannily, Norm even smelt a bit like the twin towers. Every night we stayed out late, not returning home until a foolish lofted punt had lost the ball on to a rooftop. On one memorable occasion we didn't get back until it was almost dark!

In those days talent scouts would criss-cross the country in search of young talent, and it wasn't long before I was spotted and given my chance. At first I turned them down – I wasn't going anywhere without my new friend – but when Norm's mother called him in for his tea, I took the bull by the horns and jumped at it!

My football career was underway. What a baptism of

fire! I was thrown straight in at the deep-end – turning out as a scheming inside-forward for Yeovil's reserve youth team. And what a début – causing mayhem as I jinked round the Grimsby defenders, the ball glued to my foot, quite literally. But it was to be the first of many false dawns, leading to a rather humiliating incident in the fifth minute, when the adhesive gave out just as I was careering through their packed defence, still continuing on my mazy run, quite unaware that the ball had bobbled off into touch.

And that was it, Ron's a goner*! My crestfallen expression said it all – 'Bollocks'. (Don't worry you young 'uns, there's a glossary somewhere.)

With my hopes and dreams shattered, I left the stadium before the half-time interval, inconsolable, not even stopping to pick up my bag. Yet as I trudged despairingly through the dead-end streets of this backward shanty town, I heard the familiar sound of breathless wheezing and clumping footfall – it was Big Norm with my holdall! Flinging a reassuring, if frankly unhygienic, arm around my shoulder, he spoke the words that would sustain me throughout my long and glittering career.

'Don't take it hard, Ron. You was never up for it.'

And despite the evidence of my mother's carefully prepared half-time buns tucked in the fleshy crevices of his wan smile, I knew that here was a true friend.

I returned home with my tail between my legs, and spent the next year working furiously with my stamp collection and helping out at the local donkey sanctuary, building

---

* Ron's ass was out of there.

friendships which would influence my later life. 'Two-legs' Neddy – God rest his soul* – he taught me humility and self-esteem, like him I would learn to stand on my own two feet – me and Bert had inadvertently talked Neddy's hind-legs off while furiously debating the merits of the Christmas-tree formation.

At that point in my life I could have taken a completely different road, depriving the world of football of one of its most influential influences (if that's allowed). But then, one night, as the whole family gathered round the old crystal set – Waterford, according to my brother Tom, who had 'thieved' it – there was a knock at the door and completely out of the blue, I was presented with the contract which took me into the world of professional football. And I returned to Craven Cottage – this time the door was open.

At last my professional career had begun. Three years of cleaning, scraping, polishing the boots of the big-headed, pampered prima donnas of the maximum wage – marvellous.

And I was back at Wembley much quicker than I expected. Good old Uncle Bert! A spare ticket for Burnley against Charlton, the FA Cup final, 1947. And this time, what memories! Wasn't it? Ho ho, er.

The ball burst!

While weeing against the twin towers I promised Uncle Bert that I would one day win that FA Cup medal for great-uncle Bill.

---

* Ron's ass is history.

CHAPTER THREE

THE FABULOUS FIFTIES

It's just a round thing you kick to another player, hmm?
Isn't it? . . . What is it? . . . Er . . .

WHO is Ron Manager, hmm? I've asked myself many a time. I even had to ask the wife once. It all depends who you ask, really. One fellow thought I was Rummenigge – though I was slurring a little at the time.

Well, you young 'uns probably know me merely as a top television personality, but you go and ask your dad, I bet you he'll remember Ron!

'Er, wasn't that Fulham's tough uncompromising wing-half in the late fifties, son? . . . Wait a minute . . . Wasn't he Hartlepool's scheming inside-forward in the mid-fifties? . . . Torino's machiavellian midfield misfit maestro of the mid-sixties? . . . Ah . . . The caretaker-manager of Grimsby at the height of Beatlemania? . . . Hang on, didn't he score that wonder goal dribbling through the whole of the Argentine defence before unleashing a screamer into the roof of the net?'

Ho ho! Put a sock in it, Pops! Once you get the dotty old bugger started, you'll never shut him up! But that was Ron all right, every one of them – from Fulham to Grimsby and all stops in between. (Obviously not the screamer into the Argy net, but don't disillusion the daft old coot. Whose memory doesn't occasionally play tricks on them as the years roll by? Hmm?)

But yes, and what a long, strange trip it's been. It seems like only yesterday* I was rushing through the streets after making my professional début at right-back for Fulham, haring round to my Uncle Bert's news-stand, eager to catch the match report in the pink paper, the *Late Sports Extra*.

Don't suppose any of you young 'uns remember the 'old pink 'un' either – the *Late Sports Extra* I mean, not my Uncle Bert! No, the hastily written sports paper on sale within an hour of full-time whistle. That long ago Saturday's headline is still as vivid in my mind today** as it was that evening***.

'Hail the Hat-trick Hero!'

Not me, actually, Bob Hail, the opposition centre-forward that day – though in years to come, I often went home with the match ball – quite inadvertently!

Bloomin' Bob Hail ran me ragged, literally. Turned me inside out, laterally! I didn't know if I was coming or going,

---

* Thursday.
** Friday.
*** Saturday evening long ago.

literally. Talk about a baptism of fire! Five minutes into the game, I realised that the right-back position which I'd latterly adopted was not my forte, literally. And so I reverted to my customary role as a scheming inside forward, oblivious to the 'gaffer' doing his pieces on the touchline as his game plan unravelled before his eyes. But it certainly gave me an early insight into the way a tactically astute manager can turn a game round with just a few minor tweaks. And remember there were no such things as substitutes in those days. Eventually, after a few minutes humming and hawing, quite literally, as he did his pieces on the touchline, the gaffer took me off anyway and I spent the rest of the match scheming furiously on the bench. In many ways you could call me the original 'super sub'.

It always makes me laugh reading about the young lad Solskjaer getting 'the right hump' – if that's not putting it a bit strongly – belly-aching at being typecast just for having the knack of coming off the bench to score timely goals. The manager knows best! And if you earn a nickname, you're getting yourself noticed. I was known for suddenly raising myself from my torpor to pop one in at the last minute – though you never knew at which end! 'Consolation Ron', wasn't it, hmm?

Mrs Manager still calls me it – and she never knew at which end it was going to be either. Marvellous!

Ho ho! er, where was I? Yes! Undeterred by the disappointment of my début, I went back to basics and re-invented myself as a bone-crunching centre-half. And it wasn't long before I was making the headlines myself, proudly picking up the 'old pink 'un' at Uncle Bert's news-stand . . .

'As a bone-crunching centre-half, all that is missing from Ron Manager's game is the bone-crunching.'

And now, with my first press cutting proudly pasted in the old scrapbook, I was Charlie Big Potatoes! My mother's still got it somewhere, though now yellowed with age – not my mother – the cutting in the scrapbook! – treasured memories of a golden age lost forever.

Not long ago I shuffled out of a dismal top-of-the-table tussle at Maine Road ten minutes before the whistle, confidently expecting to bone up on the day's results in the *Late Sports Extra* on the train home. I arrived at the station minutes before departure, only to be told the old pink paper's folded!

Ron, is that one of your funnies?

Eh?

Lad culture, that's what's to blame. Nowadays if you want to read about football it's the glossies, monthly magazines full of sex and innuendo. Without wishing to appear old-fashioned, it's not like the thrill of getting hold of the 'old pink 'un' on a Saturday evening. Had to make do with a copy of *FHM* and, without wishing to appear in any way prudish, what on earth is all this kerfuffle about that Kylie Minogue? She doesn't even have a . . . well, you know, a 'posterior'. In my day we preferred our womenfolk to be a little more curvaceous. And we expected them to keep their curves under wraps. Be fair, let's doff our hats to the Taliban on this one. Not you, ladies! – ho ho – marvellous.

Er, where was I? Oh yes, Fulham. My introduction to the world of professional soccer. Treasured memories! Team spirit! 'One for all and all for one!', 'in for a penny . . .' Isn't it? 'Backs to the wall!' Marvellous!

What a team! That was the team that was, wasn't it? Mickey Nip, Sol Pardew, Eddie Cleak, Chris Pipe, Bob Nudge, Cliff Richards, Terry Pop – legendary names, hmm?

Bert Howe! What a pairing we made as a twin-pronged attack in the inside-forward position – now perhaps lost forever to the beautiful game. Bert 'The Howitzer' Howe, wasn't it? Left leg like a small-barrelled cannon with a low-muzzle velocity in deadly harness with Ron 'Blunderbuss' Manager – right leg like an obsolete short musket. And, let me assure you, I always had my finger on the trigger.

Was I the original 'Dead-eye Dick of the Six-yard box'? Modesty prevents me from accepting all the compliments paid to me over the years. I'll meet you halfway! Take out the 'dead-eye' bit, and that was Ron Manager in his pomp, hmm?

And the memory plays tricks as time goes by. For every shot that went in, maybe a dozen came back off the woodwork. Don't forget, that was when they used real wood, not that bendy stuff they make corner flags out of today.

But legendary names one and all, I can still recite them like a litany, literally. Legendary players! And at the hub of it all was Sid 'Squeaky' Stein, our club captain. A mild-mannered journeyman signed on loan from Buckie Thistle, made captain after 'Bustling' Bob Nudge had sustained a minor injury blundering into the tea urn at half-time.

Sometimes that extra responsibility can completely change a player. Look how shy, retiring, bit-part player David Beckham was transformed when he first took the captain's armband from an injured Roy Keane at Old Trafford. Yet, here's a bit of inside gossip for you, this defining moment for English football was all due to a bit of a misunderstanding between two top footballing brains. Keano had pulled up lame in the mistaken belief he had an Ireland friendly that week and Becks has pulled on the armband thinking he's bagged a lovely garter to wear with Victoria's hosiery.

Ho ho! Becks, isn't it? Exquisitely talented, hmm? Always dangerous at set-plays, often bewilderingly coiffed, but he's blossoming into being England's finest skipper since Alan Ball!

But it just goes to show that you don't need a captain with a big gruff voice. Remember 'Squeaky' Stein, hmm? Normally just an irritating anonymous cog in Fulham's midfield machine, but given the responsibility of captainship*, he was transformed into a fearsome man. Squeaky was lubricated, literally – you wouldn't believe what went into the half-time tea in those days! Er, you wouldn't, actually.

One memorable afternoon, we came in at half-time trailing by three goals to nil, down to ten men. This time the gaffer left the talking to the cap'n. There was no

---

★ Captainment.

bawling from Squeaky, no flying teacups, just that calm menacing peep. 'Pull your socks up! . . . Roll up your sleeves!' Ho ho! We all got the general drift. As we took to the field for the second half, I even tucked my shorts into my underwear, only to be promptly dismissed for lewd and offensive behaviour – marvellous.

But I was beginning to get noticed. And my first nick-name of many – Ron 'Pants' Manager. Marvellous!

But be fair, a motivational team captain can make all the difference between drawing or losing. Squeaky Stein was a winner, and even if the rest of us weren't, we stuck doggedly at it – literally. And under Squeaky, I was beginning to find my touch! – That sounds a bit odd, doesn't it? But when he told you to get your finger out, you did.

Ron Manager in his pomp! First in the tackle, first to the tea urn at half-time, bustling in midfield, policing the halfway line, mildly bloated from the half-time tea – but unless answering a call of nature, nothing would make me leave the pitch.

I remember once struggling on while carrying a terrible injury, yet the roars of the crowd spurred me on to ever greater exertions. It was only later that I was informed that most of their applause had been actually directed at a small dog. Ho ho! Spent most of the first half scooting up the touchline and attempting to mate with the linesman – the dog, not me! – but a dogged performance nonetheless. Er, me, not the dog! Well, both of us, I suppose.

But that was Ron Manager in his pomp. Wouldn't leave the pitch till I was carried off. It finally took three players, two members of the constabulary and the peanut vendor. Marvellous! Even then I was back for the second half.

But in among all the personal triumphs, there's always going to be a few low points. Well, we've all got one – it's the way we're built, literally. Ho ho! – I'm laughing out loud here!

Joan, send this off to Kenny Lynch.

For me the worst times were towards the end of my career at Fulham in the late sixties. While they stretchered me off after a ferocious tackle on Dave Mackay, I inadvertently played the opposing centre-forward onside, and as his thunderous volley cannoned back off the bar, I made a superhuman effort, and courageously raised my head – only to weakly divert the ball off of it, into my own net.

Nowadays everybody would be bleating, 'But Ref, he wasn't interfering with play!' Let me assure you here and now, when Ron Manager was on the pitch, he was always interfering with play!

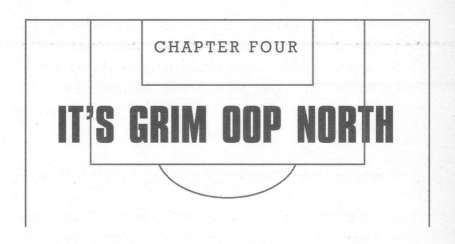

CHAPTER FOUR

IT'S GRIM OOP NORTH

Have boots, will travel. Isn't it?

THE late fifties! Rock 'n' roll! The Big Bopper! Little Richard! The Big Dipper! er, apparently. Awopbopaloobopabingbangbong, wasn't it? 'He sounds like he's got a sore belly,' I used to quip! Ho ho! Wild nights with Big Norm down at the Rivoli Ballroom in Catford. Marvellous! Little did I know, literally, but my life was about to change forever.

Though well established as a firm favourite of the crowd at Craven Cottage, the progress of my career was about to come to a juddering halt with the signing of some chinless wonder called Jimmy Hill, which eventually led to me being transferred to Hartlepool United – only bloomin' swapped! – and quite a complicated transaction in fact, involving a little Geordie no-hoper then known as Bob Robson and a holdall stuffed with used bank notes (which Fulham could scarcely afford in those austere days before the television johnnies cottoned on to the appeal of the beautiful game). The actual terms of my contract finally became the cause of some dispute, resulting in a landmark ruling by an FA tribunal which, after much humming and hawing, eventually compelled me to return the holdall.

Where was I? Ho ho! Oh yes! In many ways you might say I was the Marc Bosman of my day. Although they were then widely regarded as a toothless bunch of old, er, well, 'farts', the tribunal bit the bullet and made the decision which would send reverberations through the whole world of football. The wind of change was blowing back into the faces of the old farts – Parp! isn't it? – marvellous.

Joan, take that out – I'm just having fun.

No, leave it, Ron, I like it.

From that day on, any player who left on a 'Manager' was sent on his way clutching his 'sweetener' in a brown paper bag. Much in the way that those leaving on a 'Bosman' are today*!

For the fat-cat chairmen controlling us like pawns – or is it prawns? No, it's pawns – controlling us from their lofty perches, this was a timely wake-up call, setting the alarm bells ringing throughout the world of the beautiful game. Bells which still resonate – er, hang on, is that what

---

* Tuesday as I write this.

bells do? – which still, er, resound? – Bloomin' heck! Er, pardon my French! – What do the bloomin' things do? You know, the alarm bells which still bloomin' bing and bong through the bloomin' game today, for *uck's sake!

Joan, write down the page number, I'll sort this bit out in the morning.

And so, my crazy nomadic football wanderings had begun. But if the Fulham faithful thought that was the last they had seen of 'Craven Ron', they were sadly mistaken. Some years later, 'The Cottagers' finally realised the error of their ways and enticed me back. Plenty of players have returned to a club for a second time. A backward step? – Guff! Home is the hero!

Anyone remember Denis Law? Sold by Manchester City to Torino only to be brought back to Blighty by Manchester United, where he languished in the penalty area for a number of seasons before being offloaded unceremoniously and sold back to City, the 'pride of Manchester's' then little-known neighbourhood rivals! Confusing hmm? But it was Denis's deft back-heel in the dying minutes of a local derby that was to send the mighty Reds tumbling into the lower divisions.

Eerie parallels with Ron Manager in the pomp of his twilight years, isn't it? – marking my return to Craven Cottage by scoring the goal which condemned my first-ever club to relegation. The moment made doubly poignant by the fact that I'd only recently re-joined them on a free transfer.

But, hang on a minute, 'Hold your horses, Ron!' I'm getting a bit ahead of myself here. Where was I? I could have been anywhere. 'Ramblin' Ron Manager' they used to call me – not because I used to witter on or anything – ho ho! – No! because of my crazy 'football' ramblings. Mind you, 'Wittering' Ron was an occasional soubriquet as well.

Have boots will travel, isn't it, hmm? Although I may have been surplus to requirements at Craven Cottage, there was no shortage of clubs eager to secure the services of Ron Manager and so after a fierce bidding war, I was off-loaded to the 'monkey-hangers' in exchange for a box of kippers.

And as a sophisticated Londoner, my first experience of the Northeast was quite a culture shock. Everybody was thick! And as for the food? – hmm? shocking! After a week I would have swapped all the butties and barm-cakes in the world for a tub of jellied eels and a meat pie slobbering with liquor. But on the pitch it didn't take long for me to find my feet. Ho ho! Cometh the hour, cometh Ron Manager! At the time then relatively unknown outside my own manor, here was a whole new box of tricks, exploding on to the scene much in the way Johan Cruyff, Maradona or even the young lad Beckham would in years to come. Though in the same way as those other maverick young talents, my initial effectiveness was somewhat short-lived, and a succession of bewildering barnets was not an option in those less permissive days hmm?

On the terraces and in the press, heated debate ensued. Was I a flash in the pan or was I merely suffering a dip in form? Or, much like the future England captain, had opponents just 'sussed' how to deal with me?

Becks, hmm? Isn't it? In many ways England's play-maker is so uncannily reminiscent of the young Ron Manager in his pomp, it gives you the willies! Bloomin' eerie! So many similarities, wasn't it? Like him I burst on to the scene, a precocious talent causing mayhem among defenders unaccustomed to my game – bamboozling oppo-nents! taking up threatening positions on the left, turning up unexpectedly on the right, tearing down the wing, a change of pace, a little shimmy – hmm? – then an unex-pected change of direction – drop of the shoulder, fol-lowed by that sudden burst of speed as I went storming through the middle causing utter confusion as I hared towards goal! – marvellous! But eventually opponents got wise to me and three games into the season, most of them tended to leave me to my own devices and concentrate on the player with the ball.

Yet despite finding myself once again a square peg in a round hole, I never lost the affection of the crowd. What supporters they have in the Northeast! And in those days you'd travel to the game on the same bus as them. Bloomin' terrifying! And though my time in this little-known soccer backwater was destined to be short-lived, I've always retained a deep affection for that bunch of ill-educated, in-bred, half-witted hoodlums from the, er, 'Arsehole of Britain', as it's affectionately known down south. Marvellous!

In many ways I was the original soccer chameleon – ho ho! – Hang on a minute . . .

Joan, didn't I have one of my 'funnies' to bung in here? You know, all that 'red' Ron, 'yellow' Ron stuff? No? Well don't get rid of it yet, just in case we're going to end up a bit short. I'll think of something.

Oh yes! That was Ron Manager in his pomp. The original soccer chameleon – strong, resilient, changing colour on a whim. Er . . . long slender legs and a prehensile tail. Er . . . ferocious in the tackle, yet only once booked for ungentlemanly conduct – and that was merely for answering an unexpected call of nature in front of the family enclosure. Bloomin' little Hitlers some of those refs, even back in the good old days, hmm? Be fair, it's not as if the kids minded. They thought it was just another of the hilarious bits of prestidigitation they'd come to expect from 'Magic Ron'. And it certainly didn't affect my popularity with the fans. Any one of that Hartlepool team who managed to play a full forty-five minutes without sloping off for a leak would soon have found the hard-drinking Victoria Ground faithful questioning their sexuality! hmm?

Ron Manager in his pomp! The tenacious, tussling, yet implacably unflappable centre-half – try saying that a few times! – plying his trade in the hot-bed of football; strong as a lion, yet as cool as the mountain dew. Marvellous!

Sounds a bit like an ad for Consulate, doesn't it? I used to smoke sixty of the blighters a day. Not so much for health reasons, more to disguise the fumes from the half-time tea – pokey stuff!

But the menthol cigarette! Wasn't it, hmm? Always the

choice of the more health-conscious sportsman. Even if it meant enduring a gentle ribbing from my bluff northern team-mates – 'the Ponce' they called me. Ho ho. I took it all in good part. Thick as arseholes, the whole bloomin' lot of them. Marvellous!

And there you go, a Hartlepool story that doesn't mention that old urban myth about the townsfolk hanging a shipwrecked monkey thinking him to be a French spy*!

Ho ho! Friendly a bunch as you could shake a stick at**. Those northerner laddies might look a bit fearsome, but they're harmless – apart from the occasional murderer and such like. But, be fair, you find that in any community, hmm?

I even found myself back in their company recently after inadvertently attending a pointless Third Division tussle at Leyton Orient. After a dour ninety minutes – including stoppage time – as the O's and 'Pools fought unsuccessfully for a place in the play-offs, I sloped off for a beer, only to find myself bowling along in the company of the 'Poolie Massive'. (That's what they like to call themselves these days – don't ask me why, something to do with American gang culture, I suppose.) But forget your preconceptions – hold your horses! – a vicious bunch of half-wits, perhaps, but they're all quite small and there's hardly

---

* Legend has it that the residents of Hartlepool, finding a ship's monkey washed up on the beach during the Napoleonic War, thought he must be a French spy, so interrogated him unsuccessfully for some time before hanging him! Thick or what? Ho ho! It's grim oop North!

** Er, best not to.

any of them. (Ho ho! Just one of my 'funnies', lads! It's satire.)

But what marvellous company! Hats off to the 'Poolie Massive' – the salt of the earth! And let me tell you, they can certainly put it away.

One of them had a lovely little dog on a length of string, and having bent down to pat it on the head – purely out of politeness, I assure you – he's insisted on giving it to me. Well, I'm not a big animal-lover, but – ho ho! – those big googly eyes – why not! And the little fellow was great company on the long walk home – I became quite attached to him! – only to arrive on my doorstep to a frosty reception from Mrs Manager. 'Ron, it's a monkey and it's not alive.'

CHAPTER FIVE

THE SWINGIN' SIXTIES

'Either you've got the ball or they have. What? . . .
Neither of us have . . . Er . . . Where is it then?'

THE early sixties! Swinging London! Er, 'rock 'n' roll'!
Wasn't it? The Big Beat! The Big Bopper! Little bloomin'
Richard! 'Bebop-a-bloomin'-lula', isn't it? 'Awopbopaloo-
bopabloomin'bingbangbong' – it wasn't? Wild nights with
Big Norm down at the Rivoli Ballroom in Catford!
Beatlemania might have been sweeping the country, but
back then we thought it was just a passing fad. Down at
the Rivoli, it was business as usual. After getting his fingers burnt buying up the Beverley Sisters' back catalogue
from Wolves skipper Billy Wright, the DJ's reluctance to
splash out on any of the Mersey Beat discs then rocking
the nation was entirely understandable. And, let me tell
you, that didn't bother 'Rockin'' Ron Manager one, er,
'whit'?

Joan, check what a 'whit' is.

I'd lately mastered the hully-gully and besides, in comparison to my rock 'n' rollin' heroes, I found the loveable moptops' irresistible blend of earthy Scouse humour and a pounding beat, well, a load of 'guff', actually.

'It sounds like they're all suffering from trapped wind,' I used to quip!

Little did I know the Fab Four would prove as enduring as the hula-hoop and the pogo-stick! Overnight the swinging sixties had arrived – mini-skirts, dolly-birds, earthy blooming Scouse humour, Tarby! 'Wor' Cilla! Roger Miller! 'England swings like a pendulum do . . .' Eh? er, isn't it?

What a time to be a young man in the prime of life! And that's where I found myself, slap bang in the middle of my pomp. But storm clouds were already gathering over the English game and, with the strictures of the maximum wage, many of us were already gazing wistfully, with furrowed brow, at the inflated wages enjoyed on the Continent, and tales of the playboy lifestyles enjoyed by the fancy Dans of Serie A. And as they climbed into their Ferraris and Lamborghinis, often with Gina Lollobrigida, we knew they were bloomin' laughing at us!

The winds of change! Wasn't it? – Even the FA big-wigs knew something was brewing! Let me tell you, us English lads were getting disgruntled.

Joan, check what disgruntled means. I think I had a 'fart joke' to go with it. If I think of it I'll try to bung it in later.

But yes, it was time for someone to make a stand. Unaccustomed as I was to public speaking, I stood in front of my disgruntled comrades, and I let rip! – marvellous! Cometh the hour, cometh Ron Manager! On his soapbox – till some bl*ghter nicked it. Revolution was in the air. Something had to give – and eventually it was Ron's banana box, a flimsily constructed affair I'd commissioned to replace my soapbox.

Ho ho! I was a bit of a firebrand in my youth, you know. 'Shorter hours! Longer shorts!' 'One out, all out!' 'Cultured left leg in, cultured left leg out!' Marvellous.

'Red Ron' they used to call me. For a while I even sported the Che Guevara moustache, with just a hint of 'light goatee' – though, obviously, being still in my late twenties, I had to enhance it slightly with a touch of mascara. Ho ho! Some of it must have rubbed off on my Fulham nemesis Jimmy Hill – er, my revolutionary spirit I mean.

Always a traditionalist at heart, I was reluctant to rock the boat. I preferred to keep my thoughts to myself, but Jimmy took the ball and ran with it – much like Harry Whatsit in his pomp – turning the football world on its head and sowing the seeds of the inflated salaries of the pampered, wife-beating professionals of the modern game which would bring the game to its knees in the twenty-first century. Marvellous!

And let me let you into a little-known secret here – I can't reveal too much, us footie folk have an unwritten code you know (don't ask me what it is, because I've never read it), but breaking my vow of silence, if you like – Jimmy's beard, which would later afford him that air of 'gravitas' necessary for football punditry, was originally created by dunking that famous chin in a tub of gravy browning! Ho ho! There's a bit of gossip for you – helps bump up the serialisation fees from the tabloids, hmm? We all do it – it's the unwritten football code!

Er, back to the early sixties and yes, the champagne lifestyle ushered in by the abolition of the maximum wage turned many a young man's head. One week we were taking home a mere twenty nicker, then suddenly, Johnny Haynes, the 'Brylcreem boy', was picking up a monkey . . . or was it a pony? er, whatever it was, in those days it was a lot of lolly, literally. Try saying that a few times!

Be fair, we didn't all earn quite that much, but football changed overnight. For young men suddenly with money to burn, Saturday night meant a dad of goose fat in the old barnet and off to Catford to trip the light fantastic and put it about a bit. And with a couple of glasses of milk stout under my belt, I was buzzing. I was Charlie Big Potatoes!

Is there anything wrong with a hard-working young sportsman occasionally letting his hair down? 'Work hard, play hard', was always my motto – not that I was a hell-raiser, mind you, I just found them both really difficult.

But alcohol was not my particular poison back then! Personally, I used to spend the extra ten bob in my wage packet on 'Do-do tablets', 'as recommended by Mrs B. of Bristol' in the back pages of the Sunday papers. An over-the-counter stimulant, wasn't it? And all perfectly legal, I hasten to add. Marvellous! A couple of Mrs B.'s little beauties at half-time and I was up for anything – prowling the midfield like a caged tiger, flying down the wing like

an antelope with its arse on fire, popping up unexpectedly in the six-yard box like – well, like some sort of small
burrowing mammal I suppose*.

Ho ho! Powerful stuff! and not without a few side-effects
– fierce buzzing of the scalp – strange shrivelling of the
extremities. What the heck, I was Charlie Small Potatoes!
I soon got used to a gentle ribbing in the team bath . . .
Er hang on, where was I?

Yes! – in many ways the sixties was a decade of two
halves, each roughly of five years' duration. The 'permissive society', wasn't it? Hmm? And it wasn't everybody's cup of tea. To be honest, in the early years most
of us footie folk were dead set against it. Little did we
know that the loony causes such as 'women's lib', so vocif-
erously espoused by the loony lefties, would eventually
deliver such memorable moments as Erica Roe bouncing
joyfully across the pitch at Twickers! We were content
with our lot, and if we'd had even the merest inkling of
'free sex', we would have thought that 'loony' too. And
the very notion would have certainly nipped Jimmy Hill's
campaign against the maximum wage in the bud!

But from tiny acorns, mighty oaks do grow, hmm? The
world of football was opening up and soon the European
clubs started to take an interest in the wealth of talent
blundering aimlessly in the birthplace of football. They
were finally waking up to the benefits of adding a little
English backbone to their spineless, languid, foppish game.

And though us English lads were initially a little wary

★ Perhaps a marmoset.

of the prospect of plying our trade amongst . . . well, a bunch of pansies, I suppose – but the lure of the lira, the pull of the peseta, the scent of the centime, the draw of the drachma, the call of the wild, the cancan and the Folies Bergères hmm? We was right up for it – marvellous!

And learning my trade alongside and against some of the 'greats' in the more 'manly' days of the fifties had given me an edge of steel that set me apart from the long-haired, mincing playboys who were now coming into the game. Bert Sugar! Boothby Swipe! Patsy Potter! 'Desperate' Dan Cortshort! Reg Dwight! Names perhaps less familiar than the Stanley Matthewses and the Stanley Mortenseneses of that era, but the little tricks, those little bits of finesse that I picked up, hmm? The trap, the quip, the little flick to the nuts of the opposing forward as he rises for the ball in a crowded six-yard box, the sly kick in the wotsits as you disentangle from a sliding tackle, the cynical stamp on an opponent's leg as you emerge after clattering into the advertising hoardings, the quick tweak of the bovrils. Marvellous!

And just as the Italian moneymen were waking up to what was missing from the Continental game, so were the stout yeomanry from the home of football cottoning on to the rich pickings to be had for little effort across the water.

Dawneth the wops, dawneth the under-paid stars of the English league – many of them only to 'dusketh' some-what rapidly owing to the tempo of the spineless, languid, foppish game in Serie A. Marvellous!

As for Ron Manager? I had other fish to fry, literally.

CHAPTER SIX

HO HO . . . ISN'T IT?

'Hello. What are you doing? Are you dancing?'

'Are you asking?'

'Only out of concern, Ron.'

THERE comes a time in every young lad's life when his natural fear of girls becomes compromised by insatiable lust. Women, isn't it? Bloomin' marvellous!

Looking back I realise I'd always had an eye for the ladies. But like so many young men I found them terrifying – and I don't mean just those burly big lumps you get up North! No, even the sweet little boyish ones down in the more civilised, sophisticated South.

Well we all used to fall for the 'waif', didn't we? Ho ho! Not the 'trouble and straif!' – but there's something about those boyish, gamine young women that fires the soul of the poetic tender-souled young fellow, that has you turning cartwheels and composing tender love sonnets in their honour, that makes you want to put your arm round them and say reassuringly, 'It's all right, Reg.'

Naturally, as the years rolled by, I tended to go for the 'fatter bird'. Be fair, we all do, don't we?

My Uncle Bert used to tell me, 'It's all right having an eye for the ladies, as long as you keep your eye on the ball!' – taking him at his word, I inadvertently found myself dating 'Boss-eyed' Bertha Juggins, who pursued me doggedly, if mistakenly, as a kindred spirit.

But back then, if any woman in the world, from Bristol to the Norfolk Broads, had even asked me my name, I was reduced to jelly, literally! Tongue-tied and stammering like a callow thirty-year-old.

Ho ho! The Norfolk Broads, isn't it? Carrow Road! 'Ar you roight boy?' Lilie Ferrari, wasn't it? Chassis like a Hillman Imp! Ho ho! Marvellous!

Ron, you never mentioned her.

Er, I'm sure I did. Hang on.

Yes! – I met up with her again just recently when taking part in a charity version of *Ready Steady Cook*. Narrowly eliminated in the first round of the egg-boiling after a ferocious head-to-head with Delia Smith, I was just oiling my pans before stowing them back in the car when I heard that familiar voice, '. . .'Ev' you got a loight, boy?'

I spun round to see that familiar, vicious, narrow-eyed

look of recognition. "'Ere, aren't you that Ron M-m-m-m-m-anager?'

Suddenly once more I became that tongue-tied adolescent – I was so distracted I nearly oiled my pans for a second time! M-m-m-m-m-m-arvellous!

But as my career burgeoned, so did my self-confidence. And my social circle broadened overnight! Ask Big Norm! Suddenly I was Charlie Big Potatoes!

I'd led a sheltered youth – never a toper, nor 'bonviveur' but my new celebrity lifestyle introduced me to the heady world and the heightened emotions of the devil's brew – 'the Drink'.

And so, bolstered, bushy-tailed and bleary, I now found myself strangely attracted to the fairer sex, or should I say the 'tender gender' . . . Ho ho! I made that up myself!

Er, yes, I had become strangely aware of a rather plain, shy, awkward girl called Joan, who worked in the cloakrooms down at the Rivoli Ballroom. Little did I know that this dumpy, plug-ugly little thing with her buck teeth and irritating manner would one day be my ball and chain!

Ron, I presume you've got your witty hat on.

Joan had recently been promoted to the position of hatcheck girl and so I set myself to wooing her with a blinding range of 'titfers' – leather pork-pie, stovepipe – reminiscent of Abe Lincoln in his pomp, beret at a rakish angle. (Me and Big Norm used to do a little Abbot and Costello 'hat-swapping' routine to impress the girls! – blindin'!)

I threw my hat into the ring literally! and though obviously not bowled over by my fez, I caught even Joan shooting admiring glances at my *pièce de résistance* – my two-gallon hat – which I found to be actually a little under its declared capacity when caught short that night on my way home. That's when you thank your lucky stars for having a beret folded in your back pocket! hmm?

I knew I was besotted. Us chaps don't talk about our feelings very much – we bottle it up! – but walking home with Big Norm under the starlit skies, I suddenly had to unburden myself and I bared my soul and 'loosened my load' – as California soft-rockers The Eagles would say.

I'll never forget the sincerity in Big Norm's eyes as he turned to me and said, 'Ron, you was bang in there with that Joan. If you don't pull it, I'll eat my hat!'

How could I lose? And having just noticed that we had inadvertently swapped hats while regaling a couple of 'sorts' with our Abbot and Costello routine, I continued to relieve myself somewhat sheepishly, but with a light heart. Marvellous!

Courting my Joan! Dazzling her with my witty and occasionally saucy repartee – but never anything offensive! She gave as good as she got – we should have been a double act.

I remember leaving the Rivoli one night, picking up my newly acquired tricorn, doffing it flirtatiously over my left eye – reminiscent of Napoleon in his pomp – and in the light reedy tenor I'd inherited from good old Dad, I crooned, 'My hat it hath three corners. Three corners hath my hat.'

'Ron, you've sat on it . . . It's got five.'

Marvellous! Ho ho! I'd cracked it!

We both had our own interests and obsessions – Joan knew nothing of football and I hadn't even heard of trepanning – but we were made for each other – er, possibly not literally – marvellous.

Be fair, football's a man's game, isn't it? Maybe I'd led a sheltered life, but women? It was a whole different ball game. It wasn't soccer, hmm? 'Twosey', wasn't it? It used to make me howl! Hand a woman a couple of balls and – ho ho! – she's off! Flinging them against the wall, clapping her hands, catching them, hurling them under her leg. And singing to the bloomin' things.

'Three, six, nine . . . the goose drank wine . . . the monkey chewed tobacco on the streetcar line . . .'

Ha ha ha ha ha ha ha! Isn't it? I've said it before and I'll say it again – it's a whole different ball game! But that's your womenfolk! Whole different ball game that's your womenfolk's attitude to the ball . . . game . . .

Ron, have you gone to sleep?

Eh? I had merely closed my eyes – where was I? Ball games! Yes! But whether it's space-age plastic or a ragged old tennis ball, it's all balls, isn't it? And don't expect any cheap innuendo from Ron!

But young boys, hmm? If it rolled, you kicked it! Ho ho! Imagine getting one of those little squash balls innuend–o – innuend–aaaargh, more like it, isn't it? Hmm?

Right away I knew Joan had a soft spot for me – I had

a soft one for her – crumbs! I suppose even that could be taken both ways – bloomin' heck! Sorry if you think I'm being prudish, but let me reassure you as a man of the world, if it's a *double entendre* you're after, I'll give you one!

Ron, you're not funny.

But yes, in some ways myself and Mrs Manager were the Posh 'n' Becks of our day, but unlike the cross-dressing England captain, chez Manager it was always Ron who wore the trousers. Like the residents of 'Beckingham Palace' we stoically endured the foul-mouthed chanting from the terraces – naturally obsessed with the personal* details of our private lives. Joan made our position clear – she didn't take it lying down! Heh heh!

Ron, you couldn't manage it standing up.

I suppose in more innocent times we were the John and Yoko of our day. Anyone remember our famous 'lie-in' – spending two days in bed in 1973? Er, interestingly it turned out Joan had dengue fever . . . hang on a minute.

Women love a footballing man, isn't it? Look at Sven! No tit-bit, is he, hmm? But the minute he arrived the ladies were immediately bowled over by his urbane, rakish, Continental charm, as he hared from ground to ground with his trusty side-kick Tord Grip – his eyes and

---

* Prurient.

46

ears here in England. Taking Joan along to a game one day we found ourselves seated right behind the wily Swede – and Joan's all a-bloomin'-twitter! – but who's with him? Blow me! It wasn't his eyes and ears. It's not Tord . . . Hah! it's a dolly-bird – you know – a lass! I don't know what to call them these days! . . . er, quite an enchanting young lady, anyway. Joan had read all about her in *Women's Realm*. It was Sven's girlfriend – Nancy Dell 'Olio – all *haute couture* and red lipstick! Marvellous!

Ho ho! We were agog! Well, I suppose I was more agog than Joan, who fetched me quite a clump, mistakenly suspecting me of staring down Nancy's cleavage. Well, be fair, we all were. Except for Sven, interestingly. Hmm?

Sven might have his knockers, but he's certainly a hit with the ladies! And it's not sour grapes at being personally overlooked for the England job – hang on . . .

Ron, you've just missed one of your 'funnies'.

Eh?

Well, when Sven arrived it was a 'love-in' wasn't it? The swooning press falling heads-over-heels for 'the luxuriantly coiffed Swede'? He's blooming bald! OK, there's a bit of 'hair' about him, set far back, but 'cultured', 'urbane'? 'The ruthless determination beneath the sophisticated exterior'? 'The iron fist in the velvet glove'?

Is that the way to get the England lads going, er . . . the jury's still out. Personally, my approach was always the velvet fist in the iron glove – just as effective, isn't it? – Enough.

. . . But 'the elegantly dressed England supremo'? It's a suit and tie for heaven's sake! Does no one remember 'Manager the Mod', resplendent in two-tone mohair? Or 'Ron the Swinger' in his pomp – 'the iron hoof in the velvet trousers'? I knew how to get the lads going!

And how did they make Sven the Swedish Personality of the Year? hmm? Just for looking smart and aloof? What about that weather girl?

She's not Swedish, Ron.

What about Britt Ekland then? She's Swedish! Good old Britt – that's what I call personality! She lent me a pair of Rod Stewart's trousers once, after an unfortunate incident on *It's a Celebrity Knockout!* Ho ho! 'Do ya think I'm sexy?' 'Not 'arf!' I couldn't fit into them now, mind you – Joan boiled them a little over-vigorously after an unfortunate incident when I was guesting on *Catchphrase* . . . er, marvellous!

But the crazy, giddy worlds of football and showbiz – pop music and television – they've always been inextricably linked – and vice-versa. *Man About the House*! *On the Buses*! Marvellous birds, hmm? We just couldn't pull 'em!

Except for Billy bloomin' Wright. He set the modern trend, didn't he? Married one of the Beverley Sisters – who was that midfield trio at Hartlepool in the fifties who dated Nana Mouskouri on successive nights? . . . hang on a second, it'll come to me. That's football – hmm? we're all, er, 'babe-magnets'. Opposites attract and er, vice-versa.

Yes, it's all dolly-birds and designer labels now, isn't it? Footballers' wives? We used to pluck 'em off the factory assembly line – now they come straight from the catwalk! It's all a far cry from those innocent days when I met my future 'intended to be', her legs covered in gravy-browning instead of stockings – and not because of the strictures of post-war rationing, it was the mid-sixties, actually – just one of Joan's personal things. Ahhh . . . Bisto, hmm? – marvellous!

Ah, got it! 'Browns, Seasons and Thickens' – that's the blig*ters! Browns, Seasons and Thickens – Hartlepool's midfield trio in the fifties who all dated Nana Mouskouri, every man Jack of 'em!

Ah, Joan, I've got you now! – I've remembered my Sven's 'knockers' funny!

Ho ho! Hats off to Sven! He's, er, pulled a bird with big 'knockers', isn't it? Marvellous!

CHAPTER SEVEN

THE ITALIAN JOB

'Whatsa matter you, heh? Gotta no respec'?'

THOUGH personally I had no interest in broadening my horizons – I was settled at Fulham, thank you very much! I was a big fish in a little pond, wasn't it? – But deep down I knew something wasn't quite right. Call it the seven-year itch, if you like, but somehow, something didn't sit comfortably – and it was Ron Manager! We'd never bloomin' heard of Anusol in those innocent days – let alone Bird's Eye frozen petit pois! We just went for a dod* of goose fat. It didn't stop the itching but it certainly made walking easier – marvellous.

But little did I know, my cosy football world was about to be dramatically turned on its end – literally.

An unfortunate kerb-crawling incident – well, be fair,

---

* Dad.

we've all done it, haven't we? Us football folk couldn't afford cars in those days – a minor local scandal which was luckily, if expensively, hushed up in the English press but inexplicably splashed all over *La Gazzetta dello Sport* – brought me to the attention of the red-blooded lotharios abroad. And before you could say 'Walter Winterbottom', I was on the plane to Italy.

Rome! Wasn't built in a day, was it? It's hardly the Italian way, is it? The 'eternal city'! – 'The infernal city!' I used to quip. Ho ho! Nobody used to laugh, but I just put it down to the language barrier. It was only in later years that I came to realise that in fact it wasn't actually remotely humorous, and reluctantly erased it from my collection of 'funnies'.

And so to Lazio and *la dolce vita*. And what a culture shock! Isn't it . . . hmm?

The trains ran on time – only joking! – but it's a different world, isn't it? Alphabetti spaghetti! Linda Lusardi – *bellissimo*! The Italian Job! – well, it's extortion, isn't it? *Catenaccio*! – it's a sausage apparently. Baloney! – er, that's definitely a sausage, isn't it? Marvellous!

But what an atmosphere in the stadiums – the ear-splitting, intimidating sound of klaxons. It all seemed a long way from Blighty and the deafening ratchet of the old wooden rattle, isn't it, hmm?

Whooosh! A firework arcs across the night sky . . .

'Oh, someone's thrown a smoke flare! Man overboard! Man the lifeboats!' I used to quip to the utter bemusement of my team-mates. Bloomin' humourless bunch, your eyeties.

I often wondered where your foreign supporters got hold

of that kind of thing. It's not as if you could filch your smoke flares from the cheerily vandalised toilets of the old 'football special' on the way to the game as you could the traditional 'toilet tissue' of the English game hmm?

Izal, though, that was the stuff! Anyone remember it? Cut through the air like a knife. Chafed a little, didn't it?

What on earth was wrong with the old toilet rolls? Have we become a nation of softies? Two-ply? Why? Kleenex Double Quilted? Bah! I'm proud to say that Mrs Manager won't have it in the house.

In those days Europe was uncharted territory. To us English lads, 'foreigners' meant one thing – and one thing only! – duplicity and perfumed ponces! The foreign disease, isn't it? hmm? What on earth do our womenfolk see in these swarthy, oily, hairy little fellows?

But it wasn't just the football that was different! Rome's club a-go-go! It was a far bloomin' cry from a Saturday night out with the lads in Swinging London. And although 'The Lavender Rooms' in Soho might have seemed a little racy to some of the young 'uns in the team – many of them still barely in their thirties – but at least it was all good, clean, innocent fun. Wasn't it?

But now it was go-go dancers dangling in cages. The glitterati! The paparazzi! Dolcelatte! Calamari! Er, Sophia Loren! 'My heart goes boom boody boom boody boom boody boom . . .' Ho ho! It was enough to turn a young man's head.

Yet despite the brevity of my Italian career, I developed a deep and lasting affection for this corrupt, backward, cowardly little country, filled fit to pop with testosterone and facial hair. And when it came to serenading my future wife? Let me tell you, a touch of the old Latino magic certainly didn't go amiss. Joan didn't take much convincing when I suggested we spend our nuptials in the eternal city – or the 'infernal city' if you like!

'When the moon hits your eye like a big pizza pie, that's *amore*,' – in a nutshell, hmm? Dean Martin in his pomp! I always thought Joan was maybe a little over-fond of old 'Dino', as she used to call him. 'Don't know what you see in the drunken bum,' I used to wittily quip through clenched teeth!

But after a few days in Rome I managed to convince her that we should take advantage of the more relaxed ambience and comparative poverty of the south. Honeymooning in the Bay of Naples with Joan, which was much like Hartlepool in fact, though hounded by the press – (who had initially mistaken me for a French spy, having spotted me wolfing down a banana while sporting the muttonchop sideburns then favoured in Rome) – we still managed to snatch a few tender moments of togetherness.

And though at the time Joan seemed a little cold towards me, as I steered our pedalo under the harbour lights – waving to the frustrated paparazzi, as she pedalled furiously round the moonlit bay with her legs pumping like pistons – how I was beginning to succumb to the charms of this muscular little troll!

Even my 'ball and chain' now looks back on it as our magical years, but we all see the past through rose-tinted spectacles, hmm? Literally!

And I couldn't help noticing Joan come over all misty-

My first...
my last...
my ball and chain...
my Joan... as she was then...

... and as she is now...
'Poker?'... hmm...?

'Help mum... the food's all droopy, isn't it?' Sharing a joke with some pals outside the Parthenon.

Cutting a ug at the Rivoli ballroom, Catford, circa 1961.

'Yessir...'

'... I can boogie...'

'Sign here lads...' Inadvertently replacing my back four with the Sex Pistols.

'... boogie oogie...'

Above: Some of my old stalwarts from *Hair*. We're still in touch.

Below: Some of the lads adopt a hands-on approach to my 'Football in the Community' scheme which I pioneered while in charge of Sleepy Hollow FC.

The Bald Eagle in his pomp when he was still The Receding Eagle!

Two Big Rons... isn't it? Marvellous. But look who's clinched the 'Travolta' prize.

Above: Bowling instructions from the touchline: wind the bobbin up, wind the bobbin up...
A disconsolate Big Norm looks on.

Below: A remarkable sequence of stills, during a half-time team talk, from the Granada TV
documentary *Tactics 'n' Teacups*. Frightening... isn't it?

Manager... player–manager... doing my pieces on the touchline after surreptitiously hauling myself off!

Above: Yesss! We're not for the drop... at last.

Below: A quandary to ponder. To whom to give the half-time team talk to when managing two teams at a time. (You try saying that.)

eyed the other week*, on opening her copy of *Women's Realm* and reading of how Sven-Goran Eriksson had wooed his ferociously tenacious Nancy at a Rome night-spot on the Via Veneto. Playing footsie under the table – ho ho! – the old goat! Marvellous!

But that faraway look in Joan's eyes as the memories came flooding back of her Ron in his pomp – quite brought a lump to me, literally. I was a bloomin' dab hand at the old footsie too, you know. Enduring images, hmm?

Dinner al fresco in the eternal city – my cuban heels mercilessly caressing her open-top sandals – Joan's eyes like two limpid pools as I bawled sweet nothings over the ceaseless racket of Vespas and Lambrettas. Then, for a moment, it was like the whole world had stood still, leaving just me and Joan and the moonlight, and I gazed into her eyes like a young Cary Grant, before delicately hoofing her halfway across the piazza, still clutching her chicken-in-a-basket. Marvellous!

But Italy, wasn't it? After a couple of appearances at Lazio, I'd earned myself quite a reputation. They'd never seen anything like Ron Manager!

Understandably bemused at how my bewildering skills might best be exploited, they sent me out on loan to their hated northern rivals, Torino. 'Mamma mia! Here I go again!' Isn't it?

And unsurprisingly, I soon became a firm favourite of the Torino *tifosi*** – utterly enthralled by the sight of

---

* I'm sorry, I have no idea when it was. Maybe around the second week in June.
** The eyeties that support Turin.

uncompromising English grit among the fancy Dans of Serie A. Could Ron hack it? Not much! I wasn't going to come up short. Dogged determination pitted against silky skills – hmm? Er . . . much like my honeymoon in fact . . . marvellous!

Even back then the Italian game was a whole new kettle of tactical fish. A burly English centre-half, ambling about and occasionally kicking surreptitious lumps out of you? – fair game! . . . but nothing had prepared me for – 'man-to-man marking'.

For the duration of an Italian Cup game against Roma, I had a swarthy little fellow with a handlebar moustache follow me everywhere, literally! – quite taking the enjoyment out of my half-time wee. Giuseppe 'the Limpet' Ciccone, he was called. The bu*ger stuck to me like one of those shellfish you get stuck to the bottom of your boat – whatever they're called*.

And don't forget he was up against one of the slipperiest customers in the game. Here was a player who could find an opening in the tightest of spots – Ron 'the Winkle' Manager in his pomp. Marvellous!

Yet by the final whistle this irritating little chimp had earned my grudging respect. I never managed to give him the slip – we swapped shirts at the end of the game and I ended up with the one I started with! He still keeps in touch, does Giuseppe, and it always makes me laugh when I answer the old 'blower' and hear that voice.

★ Barnacles.

'Ron? . . . Eez Giuseppe.'

'Eh? Who? Joo – seppy?' Ho ho! Cracks me up every time!

No kidding, that's what it sounds like when he says it! Marvellous!

But for all those doom and gloom merchants who would tell you that English football had fallen behind the Continentals? – Guff! For me, the slower pace of the foreign game gave me the chance to display the full repertoire of tricks I had perfected on the cobbled streets of Potters End. – And all without some thick-eared clod kicking my arse up into the stand.

And what skills I had! Yet I was never ostentatious – though arriving without fanfare, I could land the ball on a sixpence. Has anyone other than Ron Manager ever really tried to land a ball on a sixpence? Without blowing my own trumpet I could do it ten times out of ten – or three out of ten if I did have to blow my own trumpet. Marvellous!

Cool as a cucumber – Ron 'Il Zucchini' Manager *al pompo*!

They used to say my feet were like clubs – golf clubs, not club-feet! I was reckoned to have a three wood, a wedge and a putter on each foot. In those days it was as good as having an extra leg! . . . Er reminiscent of Rolf Harris in his pomp.

The arrogance of youth! Isn't it? Remember I was still in my early thirties – lithe as a young gazelle, yet wily as an old tom-cat. Ron Ivanhoe Manager marking his territory in the world of football – marvellous! – with the confidence borne out of sheer ability. I knew I could do anything with a ball – make it perform? – I could even make it blooming talk! – thanks to a few ventriloquism lessons from a young fellow who used to turn up mysteriously at training, Roger de Courcey or something.

Ho ho! – I'll never forget the goalie's face as he shaped to dive for another of my famous 'daisy-cutters', only to watch in astonishment as the ball whistled over the crossbar with a quick burst of 'Colonel Bogey' . . . marvellous! I still chuckle when I recall his look of astonishment as it nestled into row Z with that faint little cry, 'Gottle of geer . . . Gottle of geer!' Marvellous! The Torino *tifosi* were utterly nonplussed – maybe it lost a little in the translation.

To be fair, I never really did get to grips with the language, but I did my talking on the pitch! 'Whatsa matter you, heh?' But football's football wherever you are, isn't it? And even if the football in Serie A is often likened to a game of chess compared to the blood and thunder of the English game, it's the sight of a bunch of drunken louts punting a pig's bladder around that still makes the Premiership the most popular league in the world today! – Correct me if I'm wrong!

Ron, do you mean that?

No.

Well, that was my Italian adventure and although the press had predicted that I'd return with my tail between my legs, let me tell you I returned with it firmly 'upside my head'! Within the fortnight . . . with a grudge match against Napoli looming . . . I remembered the old saying – 'See Naples and die!' Eh? Eff off, Luigi – I'm off back to Blighty!

CHAPTER EIGHT

BACK HOME

'Arrivederci Erchie!' Isn't it?

BY the mid-sixties I had achieved all that was possible in the beautiful game and I should have been content just to hang up my boots. Anyone in the world of football would have! – er, you know, been content to hang up their own boots, if they'd achieved what I had. Mind you, a fair number would have contentedly hung up my boots for me. But they didn't, so – what the heck! – I wasn't about to hang the bloomin' things up anyway – and I didn't! – and I still haven't! – I can't even find the bloomin' things! Strewth, where was I? Ah yes . . .

Be fair, I really had nothing left to prove after so long at the height of my profession, but there was just that little matter of the Jules Rimet trophy to be dealt with. The World Cup! Football was coming home! Ron Manager was coming home – and he was hoping there was going to be somebody in!

Should I have thought twice before swapping *la dolce vita* for the mud and nettles of perfidious Albion? Was there a method in my madness, er, for once? Ho ho! . . . The jury's still out on that one.

I'll never forget my first brush with the European game, none of us would. That little touch of European glamour rubbed off on all of us – none more so than the great Don Revie! – Leeds United wasn't it? – then languishing in mid-table mediocrity in the old Second Division.

A true football visionary was big Don! Inheriting a team of bluff, vicious Yorkshiremen, whose only ambition was to ruthlessly kick lumps out of the opposition, Don ditched their traditional colours for the pure white strip of Real Madrid, judiciously added a touch of vicious Celtic guile, and transformed them at a stroke into a sophisticated unit who would take Europe by storm as they ruthlessly kicked lumps out of the opposition in the modern, sly Continental style. And it wasn't all one-way traffic, I can tell you! Even today, if you take a stroll through Madrid's Latin Quarter, you'll still find a few bars where you can enjoy a game of bingo over a pie 'n' pea supper – so . . . er, put that in your pipe!

Where was I? Ah yes, arrivederci Roma, wasn't it? With the World Cup looming on the horizon, football was coming home – and Ron Manager tearing it up in the English First Div might have been the first name pencilled in on the national team sheet, but 'El Ronno Mangiapane' languishing in the backwaters of Serie A, hmm? Out of sight, out of mind, isn't it? And besides, having been widely tipped by the foreign press as the one player who might just swing it for England, I'd begun to find *la dolce* bloomin' *vita* some-what frustrating. I'd have bloomin' swung it for anyone – and I did! Willy-nilly! though ultimately not to my financial advantage er, obviously – marvellous!

Well, be fair, you've either got it or you haven't, hmm? And, don't get me wrong, Ron Manager had it all right. And deep down I knew if nobody else wanted it, I was bloomin' stuck with it!

So despite it meaning taking a backward step, I returned to my beloved Northeast – back to Hartlepool where I was greeted as one of their own, and welcomed with open arms. Rather than risk being hung in gleeful ignorance by the half-witted locals for my unexpectedly swarthy and hirsute appearance, I had prudently spent three weeks locked indoors out of the sun, and coughed up for a full body wax. Once bitten twice shy, isn't it? Marvellous!

Home is the hero! And this time, instead of a 'goodbye and good luck', I was granted my first testimonial by Hartlepool in recognition of my long service with the club – albeit* in two spells – and my inside knowledge of the chairman's dalliances** with the tea lady.

The 28th April '65 wasn't it? Eerily and somewhat unfor-tunately the very same day as the testimonial of that other long-serving, baggy-shorted over-rated titan of the English game, Stan Matthews.

But what a turnout that was, wasn't it? Puskas! Di Stefano! Eusebio! Denis Law! Jimmy Greaves! How much

---

* An archaic word for 'even though'.
** An archaic word for 'shagging'.

would that line-up be worth at today's prices*? Probably a good sight more than the line-up at Hartlepool! But the crowds still turned up in their er, hundred to watch a dour goalless walkabout featuring Ron's World XI – Mickey Nip, Sol Pardew, Chris Pipe, Eddie Cleak, 'Bustlin'' Bob Nudge, Cliff Richards and Terry Pop – legendary names . . . hmm? Marvellous!

But tumultuous times! – wasn't it? World Cup glory beckoned, and suddenly the whole country had gone football barmy! 'We're backing Britain!' isn't it? Well, backing England, obviously. The nation had caught the bug. We all remember World Cup Willie!

Well, be fair, we all suffered from it, didn't we? Hmm? And I was itching – er, to show my stuff!

But just as it seemed I was to enjoy my finest hour astride the world stage, destiny took me by the bovrils and crushed me in its clammy hands – I saw my hopes cruelly dashed before Sir Alf had even announced his squad. Suddenly, while in his pomp, Ron Manager was laid low with a mystery illness. And a grieving nation looked on in numb despair as dark clouds descended on their dreams. Ho ho! Great stuff, eh?

Er, sorry . . . A nation mourned as Ron Manager was carried from the field – doubled up in pain with suspected deep-vein metatarsus** – Bang on the eve of England's greatest triumph.

Yet 'it's an ill wind', isn't it, hmm? The hurt fades over

---

* A lot.
** Trapped wind.

the years, and I can now step back and accept that I wholly deserve the nation's gratitude for inadvertently paving the way for little-known West Ham journeyman Geoff Hurst to wangle his way into the football hall of fame with the brace of lucky goals which would controversially make the lads of '66 the undisputed champions of the world.

And although I eventually made a full recovery, it makes you painfully aware of your own fragility when plying your trade in the blood and thunder of the modern professional sporting arena – blundering recklessly and foolhardily around the pitch, urged on by the baying fans. But when an honest footballer sustains an injury you never forget the eerie hush that descends on the stadium.

And, of course, in those days we had none of the professional medical back-up which today's lairy fresh-faced oiks take for granted. Whatever happened to the magic sponge, hmm? We used to play top-level football well into our forties and fifties! Bert Lumbago played well into his sixties, despite an off-field lifestyle which saw him virtually crippled with gout before he reached nineteen!

Nowadays it's all club doctors, physios, St John Ambulance, little carts to whisk you off to the touchline the minute you so much as feign an injury, snake-oil merchants and mystical charlatans – all available 'on tap' in today's Premiership. At least there's still some of the old school doing things in the traditional way. Look at Bobby Robson – the wizened old sage – a shining example to all those young managers sitting in their newfangled 'treatment' rooms with injury lists as long as their arms!

Quite by accident I was actually sitting on the Newcastle

bench when their talented Greek defender Nikos Dabizas sustained the injury which would sideline him for almost a whole season. A lunging tackle – a sickening crunch – a stadium draws its breath, then the shout goes up from the dug-out.

'Quick! Dabizas!'

And in seconds the trainer's on the pitch with the magic sponge!

'It's his knee, you fool!' Marvellous.

But in many ways missing the cut for Sir Alf's hopelessly overrated squad of '66 was a blessing in disguise which would set me on my way to the second half of my glittering career. What caused this unexpected change in fortune? Well, believe it or not, a dodgy meat pie, similar to any you would expect to find sailing through the fetid air at any Nationwide ground today. A short-crust 'meat 'n' onions' which I had casually lobbed in the direction of the press box – only to watch in horror as it caught Mike 'the man with the mike' Michaels below the ear and laid him out like, er, a ninepin . . . ? Or a ninepence, or something. You know, like a sack of coal . . . er, whatever – it put him on his arse!

And so with the BBC World Service's commentator laid low, there was only one man for the job!

Ho ho, not you, Ron, was it?

Joan, just do the proofreading.

Yes, I was drafted in as a last-minute replacement and, despite it meaning I would have to forego my half-time wee, this was an opportunity too good to miss. And so, on the day of England's greatest triumph, I found myself actually in the BBC commentary box at Wembley, sitting next to the late, great Ken Wolstenholme. Ho ho! Nobody who watched the TV coverage will forget Ken's timeless remarks as Sir Alf's 'wingless wonders' finally beat the world at our own game. But with all due respect, I should point out that those who were glued to the wireless on that famous day are more familiar with the final moments of my own commentary on the World Service.

'Three–two to England . . . There's people on the pitch! . . . It must be all over! . . . Thank God for that, I'm bustin'!'

Ing-er-land, wasn't it? Once and for all the undisputed champions of the world! Wembley '66. The greatest World Cup final ever? Marvellous! You wouldn't want to sit through it again mind you – someone put a video of it on the other day – bloody awful!

But with the merest inklings of my future career fermenting in my mind, I cheerfully returned to the job in hand – taking my beloved Hartlepool to the top of the league. Heaven could wait!

Yet, as ever, my contentment was short-lived and soon afterwards I left under a bit of a cloud, which was no great surprise, as it had been peein' down since I arrived. My fate was sealed the minute I described the physio's wife as a pongid*. How was I supposed to know what it meant?

---

*See Glossary.

Touchy folk, hmm? And despite my fulsome apologies, it had been spelt out to me that my position had become untenable. Blooming cheek! As if I couldn't spell untenable!

So, after a short spell languishing manfully in the Hartlepool reserves, it was 'goodbye and good luck'. But yet again I fell on my feet, as I found myself whisked away from the Simian-hating hordes down to Third Division Bournemouth on a free transfer to play a crucial role in their relegation dogfight – Ron Manager? Ron player–manager! – taking the Bournemouthers down to the Fourth for the first time in their history. Marvellous!

But I knew the time was fast approaching when I would no longer be able to rely on my breathtaking pace and quicksilver reactions. Even the most experienced football brain is rendered powerless when pitted against some bottle-blond, fleet-footed, jug-eared, be-freckled, semi-literat, misogynistic young whippersnapper who's, er, in like Flynn! Wasn't it? Marvellous!

Time catches up with us all. It's one-touch football nowadays, and with the blistering pace of modern soccer, it's a young man's game, hmm? You know when it's time to call it a day. The frustration of the striker who knows he's lost that extra half-yard – calmly taking his time to tee up a shot, when 'whuffff' – you see the haunted expression that speaks louder than words, 'I have kicked fresh air.' The dawning realisation of the passage of time, as a lumbering defender finds the ball whisked off his foot before he can bring it under control, and the pained look that says it all – 'I have trapped wind'*.

Quit while you're winning, isn't it? Leave 'em, er, gagging for more! Marvellous!

And though still a mere boy of forty-two, I stepped off my dizzy, roller-coaster ride through the giddy hurly-burly world of football – only to be bunged straight back on! Peeved? – ho ho, initially perhaps.

Don't ask me why, but as we strapped ourselves into the car, and were hauled up the forty-five-degree iron ramp – chugging past rusted rivets and shrieking rails – in an instant I knew that my mind was made up. And as we took the vertiginous drop, and looped the loop for the second time, I raised my arms in triumphant manner, and shouted 'Waaaarrrgggh!' just like everyone else did – and I lost the contents of my trousers. Hang on . . .

Joan! That was supposed to say 'my trouser pockets'!

I thought it was one of your 'funnies', Ron.

Well, it wasn't – it was four bob, three marbles and one of my prize conkers – a bloomin' 'twoser'.

Er, and as I disembarked on that starlit night, the air thick with the heavy odour of fried onion and diesel, I took a wee on the tunnel of death – literally, not

---

* Deep-vein metatarsus.

some fancy figure of speech, I was bloomin' bustin'! –
I think I've got a bit muddled here, er, but there began
my crazy life on the spinning whirligig of the managerial
merry-go-round. 'Hot Dawg!' Marvellous!

Joan, my legs have gone all buckley and I feel a bit sick.

I told you to start earlier in the evening, you arse.

CHAPTER NINE

RON MANAGER – PLAYER–MANAGER

'Your hair's very long and silky, isn't it? My wife doesn't understand me.'

Here, hang on Joan! That's not the right quote for this chapter . . . That goes later on.

What do you mean 'my wife doesn't understand me', Ron?

Er, bloomin' heck! Hang on . . . Yes!

The way I had transformed Bournemouth by taking a more 'back-seat' role had shown the world of football that there was in fact more to Ron Manager than there actually was. Despite my reputation of still being able to 'do the business' where it mattered – on the pitch! – I was now regarded as one of the brightest emerging stars in the managerial firmament, and whenever the hint of a vacancy arose, the first name to be bandied about for the hot seat would be Ronald Ivanhoe Manager.

Ho ho! I told them all to '**ck off!' Hang on a second . . .

Joan, I told them to 'back off'. Can you turn the telly down?

Right ho! Yes! 'Back off', I told them. But destiny was calling, I could feel it tugging gently at my bovrils, and though Ron Manager was poised and prepared, I knew I was still finding my feet, and not being a complete tw*t, I wasn't about to leap in feet first, until I, er, found the bloomin' things!

Though eager to get cracking, I knew I wasn't the finished article, and I wanted to learn my trade outside the glare of the spotlight before I, er, plyed it. Though still a formidable presence on the pitch, I knew that eventually I was destined to move 'upstairs', and having somewhat naively turned down the role of caretaker–manager after a horrifying afternoon spent at B*Q, haggling over the bulk price on mops and buckets, I accepted what I thought to be the less high-profile position of player–manager.

When your name's being bandied about in the boardroom, you have to strike while the iron is hot. Looking back, it's probably the biggest mistake I ever made.

Be fair, you can't ride two horses at once – and if anyone should have known, it was Ron Manager. I'd already tried it when down on the seafront at Selsey Bill, only for one of my mounts to veer off across the sand dunes, just at the same moment as the other had taken a sudden shine

---

✱ Sorry! I just hit '✱' accidentally, it's next to '&'.

to a beach donkey in a fetching little hat! I bandied about a bit myself after that.

Charlie Big Potatoes? More like Charlie 'Bloomin' Big' Potatoes – I couldn't sit down for a week.

But what the heck! Ron Manager – player–manager! It seems to have gone out of fashion in the Premiership nowadays. It's only my opinion, but even if the cap fits, you can't wear both of them.

Players seem to move into management too quickly these days, hmm? Look at John Gregory running the London marathon – surely he should still be bustling about on the pitch!

Why is wee Gordon Strachan bouncing up and down on the touchline when he could be doing his pieces up and down the field? Why aren't these lads still out on the pitch digging deep and helping their teams, hmm? In my day we gave no thought to hanging up our boots till we were well into our forties.

The art of managing a team properly takes years of experience. Who wants to have all these young 'uns sitting in the dug-out? Take it from Ron, playing is for players, managing is for us lot!

Taking on the double responsibility of player–manager changes everything. Much as you might think yourself one of the lads as you take the field, when the chips are down, you're the 'gaffer' – and you can't stand on sentiment. Trying to play both roles takes a hard head. Fortunately, as ever, Ron ('bone-head') Manager would not be found wanting. Marvellous.

Enthusiastically embracing my new dual role, one of my

first decisions was to substitute myself, much against my wishes, ten minutes into a first-round FA Cup tie! But after constantly berating the ref who, quite justifiably in my opinion, had booked me after a few niggly fouls and a reckless lunge at the goalie, I decided to haul myself off before I got myself sent off.

I was bloomin' livid – here was my whole game-plan being wrecked by the unprofessionalism of one player – and at first I refused to go. Finally, after hurling abuse at the bench, I threw my shirt petulantly at myself and stormed off down the tunnel, only to get myself involved in a furious altercation with a pedal bin. Why can you never find a steward when you want one, hmm? I missed both the first-half goals – bloomin' typical! – but as the red mist finally lifted, I re-emerged, shortly before the interval, suited and booted, to serenely mastermind our plucky, though ultimately unsuccessful, fight-back from the dugout. Dignified and serene, the only evidence of my rush of blood – a pedal bin jammed on my right foot.

Though outwardly calm as I did my pieces on the touch-line, inside I was seething. You'll still hear my colleagues that day talk about the half-time rollicking⋆ I gave myself in the dressing room – frantically ducking hither and thither as I desperately tried to dodge the barrage of my expertly aimed teacups! – enduring image, isn't it?

Ron 'player–manager' Manager in his pomp! Marvellous!

⋆ Bollocking.

Where was I? Oh yes! A great player doesn't necessarily make a great gaffer. I did, obviously, but it takes a certain type of player, the increased responsibility isn't for everyone. What does it take? In a word, discipline and reliability.

Us lads growing up in the forties and fifties, we had it drummed into us, literally. Big Norm had 'conscientiousness' tattooed on his lower thigh! Ho ho! Only joking – it was 'I lov Janit'.

But those were stricter times, and we knew not to step out of line. Foul and abusive language on the pitch? Fair game, isn't it? Taking a dump in the ref's private facilities? Boys will be boys! But, back then, turning up a few hours late at the training ground on Monday morning meant ten laps of the pitch with something horrible and soggy on your head – if the old memory's not playing tricks!

Be fair, we're men, not machines – but we're paid to do a job, and if you're supposed to be somewhere, you've got to be there. And if you're not? You're somewhere else! And when you do get where you're supposed to be – you're probably late, or you've ended up somewhere else because you've forgotten where you were supposed to be in the first place! Ho ho! Er, where was I?

But the first rule if you want to make it in the world of professional football – even before personal hygiene – it's punctuality. In my playing days, even after a night on the tiles, I was up with the cock! lark! Even now, you could set your watch by me. Ask Joan! She always used to joke that my bladder was my alarm clock! I took it all in good part. Mind you, the joke was on her last week, ho ho! I slept right through my alarm two mornings in a row er, marvellous.

But in the same way that me and Joan now work as a team, sometimes two managers can work as a team. Dual management, hmm?

Joan! Great stuff, eh?

Blindin', Ron. (Have you been drinking?)

Dual management isn't it? The fans love it. When 'Boro supremo Steve Gibson saved Middlesbrough from the drop by teaming wise old owl Terry Venables with, er, Bryan Robson, just look how the crowds came flocking back to the Riverside. The minute Tel plumped himself down on the bench next to Robbo, Steve knew he'd put bums on seats! Literally. Rome might not have been built . . . hang on . . .

Joan, have you checked out how long it took them yet?

Rome might not have been built in a day, but the Riverside Renaissance didn't take as long as the Sistine Chapel, Michelangelo old son! And it's not just packed to the rafters with a bunch of tubby cherubs and fat birds with cellulite! Er, well, not cherubs anyway! Voilà! Master-stroke! Marvellous!

But is there ever such a thing as an equal partnership, hmm?

I was once forced into an uncomfortable dual-management

role with Big Norm, and though we all look back through rose-tinted glasses, even then, it was never fifty-fifty. With hindsight it wasn't even twenty-twenty! And that's with my reading-glasses and Joan's shaving mirror!

Norm had only recently been persuaded to hang up his boots at then fashionable Brentford, but what at first had seemed a marriage made in heaven, soon deteriorated into a ferocious tussle for supremacy.

Even without the mischievous attention of the press, we were instantly engaged in a furious power struggle, which spilled over into a notorious bout of public fisticuffs – which luckily neither of us was involved in.

Eventually the chairman had to intervene, and while outwardly pandering to Norm's delusions of grandeur, he turned to me with a reassuring wink, and the wise words, 'Ron, the back-end of a pantomime horse is often more important than the front.'

Ho ho! The wisdom of Solomon, isn't it? hmm.

So, as Norm strutted the stage I was right behind him, pulling the strings, secure in the knowledge that I was the power behind the throne.

Unselfishly I put my nose to the grindstone and let him take all the plaudits. Ron Manager just along for the ride? No way, José! I was the bee's knees – Charlie Big Potatoes – the top banana! I was the head honcho! Ho ho! Er, actually, to be honest, deep down I knew I was the horse's arse.

We struggled through a dismal Christmas season, to dwindling attendances, at which point Norm was per-suaded to resume his playing career and I was handed the reins. I had carte blanche*. Now I could show what I was made of!

And to everyone's astonishment, I let bygones be bygones, I put our personal grudges to one side, and completely rebuilt the team around Big Norm. Using his years of experience as the lynchpin, I rejuvenated the club, giving some of the lads their first-ever taste of league football.

Despite the chairman's protests at the fresh faces – 'You never win anything with kids!' isn't it? – reminiscent of my fellow pundit Mr Hansen in his pomp – And we all know how Fergie's fledglings made the self-assured Scotch sophisticate eat humble pie! Wasn't it hmm?

The press used to speak of 'Manager's Midgets' in the same breath as the Busby Babes – even if they had a fag on! And we all smoked like chimneys in those days.

The only reason Ronald Ivanhoe Manager was never spoken of in the same breath as Edson Arantes do Nascimento, was because his name was so long – it was just down to lung capacity in the end, nothing to do with him being really good and I wasn't – er – nothing to do with he being really good and I not!

But young boys, isn't it? Hmm? One minute all fresh-faced exuberance, playing in the local park – to coin a phrase, 'jumpers for goalpots' – the next? – the blig*ters are performing on the world stage! No-one will forget the Busby Babes! Doubt they'll remember Manager's Midgets mind you – bloomin' rubbish! They weren't actually young either – most of them were in their forties – they were just

---

★ White sheet.

all very short. The only fresh-faced fellow in the whole place was the b**ger who'd bagged the front end of the pantomime horse, Big Norm – who was thankfully arrested for coaching irregularities mid-season, before the 'monkey-gland scandals' were splashed all over the tabloids! – that was political correctness seventies style! And that was Manager's Midgets! And a lot of them are still playing today – mainly in panto admittedly! Marvellous!

'Oh no it isn't!'

Joan, I'll do the 'funnies'.

After that, I decided I was going to have to be my own man – Ron Manager, 'Manager', end of story – the buck stops here! Isn't it?

Though, incidentally, I should point out there are two types of dual management. A more challenging interpretation is to manage two clubs at the same time. This is something I did, quite inadvertently, in my later career. Caused untold grief when they both played each other and I had to give the half-time talk to both teams. All twenty-two of my players slunk back on to the pitch and underperformed. Their hearts just weren't in it. I didn't know whether to laugh or cry, so I gamely alternated between the two while occasionally bursting into song. Don't ask me why, but it certainly caused much bemusement among the gathered journalists. So there's a little tip for any of you young aspiring managers out there – stick to one team at a time, hmm? Enough! – Next chapter!

CHAPTER TEN

THE SENSATIONAL SEVENTIES

'D'ya wanna be in my gang, my gang, my gang? D'ya wanna be in my gang? . . . Eh? Why not? Hope your next sh*t's a hedgehog . . . hmm? Marvellous.'

THE seventies, isn't it? Glam rock! Bell-bottoms and busty streakers! Marvellous! The times they were a-changing! Er, not down the bloomin' Rivoli Ballroom in Catford they weren't – Big Norm all spangled up in his tank-top and loon pants, couldn't awopbopaloobopalopbambloomin' pull to save his life!

In many ways these were football's golden years, and though still contented with my lot on the bottom rung of the football ladder, I was forever looking higher – gazing longingly at the well-upholstered seats of the fellows clinging to the higher rungs. As a player my whole life had revolved around hoofing a ball hopefully upfield, now I was looking to extend my horizons. I had grown – not in stature perhaps, but I had broadened – considerably!

As I increasingly found myself between jobs, rather than have me spending more time with my family, Joan had enrolled me on a never-ending succession of courses at the local technical college. I was by now fluent in Dutch, had an advanced knowledge of taxidermy, had completed a course in creative writing – and had even found time to attempt my twenty-five-yard breaststroke badge, secure in the knowledge that another glamour club would come calling even as I towelled myself . . . er, up! Grimsby Town would not disappoint – marvellous.

Though determined to serve my managerial apprentice-ship in the footballing backwaters, I now felt I was treading water, looking for an outlet while going through the motions. Frustration was setting in! I had become a big fish among the minnows – forever seemingly swimming against the tide, while struggling to stay afloat.

Season after season taking the club to the brink of pro-motion only to find myself yet again cast adrift in a leaky boat, sold down the river, and done up like a bloomin' kipper! In order to further my career, I knew the time had come for Ron Manager to cast his nets wide, to take the plunge and head for the open sea and the uncharted waters of . . . I'm sorry, I'm completely lost . . . Er, I'm floun-dering a bit here – all gone a bit nautical, hasn't it? That's creative writing – nautical but nice! Great stuff!

Yes! Though still a relative novice on my arrival at Grimsby Town, I had honed my craft and single-handedly turned the ship around – only to have my contract termi-nated and be run out of town on a rail. Bloomin' sacked

– just for telling a reporter from the local newspaper that all women from Grimsby were 'bloaters'.

My remarks had been taken completely out of context. They were blown out of all proportion – the women I mean, not my remarks – but in a way it was a blessing in disguise. Call it serendipidity, hmm? – serenpidity – Call it what you bloomin' like, it was a stroke of luck anyway!

With the beautiful game for once taking a back seat, I threw myself again into a course of self-improvement. And with the local constabulary having confiscated my taxidermy tools as part of their ongoing investigation into Uncle Bert, it was back to the local swimming pool, where I suddenly had the bolt of inspiration that would influence the rest of my managerial career, and make Ron Manager a big noise in the world of football. Marvellous!

While making another plucky attempt at my twenty-five-yard badge, it suddenly came to me in a blinding flash – 'Eureka!', isn't it? Much like Archimedes in his pomp!

Joan, dig out my Eureka 'funny'.

As I felt my muscles pull ferociously against the water, I found myself pondering – if only there was a way to harness that strength, that physical fitness, what wonders might it bring to a professional footballer! Imagine hoofing the ball hopefully upfield and having someone lumbering after it – and here's the clever bit – lumbering after it at such a lick as to 'get on the end of it'. (Ho ho! Don't worry ladies, it's a footie term.)

'Eureka! Er . . . bleeeurgh . . .' Wasn't it? Amazing what

a lot of thinking you can get in as you're splashing half the breadth of a swimming pool. And as they fished me out by the seat of my trunks, still pondering, I knew my career was about to take a new direction. Upwards! It was my first life-changing experience on the end of a pole. Marvellous!

Ah yes! Ho ho! I've got it! – Archimedes in his pomp! – I've remembered my Eureka 'funny'!

Er – Archimedes 'pomped' in the bath.

And so 'The Manager Method' was born. Having been much influenced in the early days of my managerial career by the 'push and run' tactics introduced at Spurs by Arthur Rowe, and later as a keen student of the 'quick, quick, slow' tempo developed by the Brazilians, I set to work combining the two, and then I introduced my secret ingredient to the mix – physical fitness!

I took 'The Manager Method', I buffed it, I polished it, I refined it – I nearly bloomin' accidentally ate it once! – and I tailored it to the strengths of the traditional English professional game, all the while still clandestinely coaching, back behind the scenes at Grimsby! Confused? Ho ho – Let me explain! Ron Manager – 'Man of many faces!' isn't it? Master of disguise. They only rumbled me when I let my mask slip during a little horseplay in the team bath. Undeterred, I honed my strategy to perfection at Blyth Spartans, who were then languishing in the lower regions of the Northern Corinthian League. Who knows, had I then had access to the modern theatrical adhesives widely available nowadays, Grimsby might have been challenging for honours at the top of the Northern Corinthian League, rather than having a trophy cabinet which, to the best of my knowledge, still contains nothing more than my best pair of fake muttonchop sideburns and a handlebar moustache.

And there it was, 'The Manager Method' – possibly better known as 'hoof, hoof, rush', and the style still favoured by all but the top two or three in the Premiership today. Marvellous!

Where was I? Yes, I was on a roll! My managerial record now spoke for itself. And as a big fish in a small pond, I was coming to the attention of the fat cats. Any chairman of a team that found itself struggling for survival in the lofty heights of the old First Division, their first thought was 'Ron to the rescue!' And soon the word would go out from the boardroom like Chinese whispers on the old footie telegraph, 'Send for Manager!'

And the next day I would turn up ready to play my part in 'The Great Escape' to the familiar greeting – 'Where's the other three of you, then?'

By now I was well known for my legendary Houdini act. Isn't it, hmm? And yet it was not so much for my ability to steer a club from relegation. Be fair, can you name one other manager in the English game who ever attempted to paddle a barrel blindfold across Niagara Falls in skimpy trunks? Ho ho! Enduring image, isn't it? Ron Manager in his pomp! If anyone could avoid the drop, you could bet your boots it was Ron!

And as my reputation burgeoned, after years of trying to make ends meet – trying to build a team on a shoestring, strapped for cash, fighting with directors who would insist, 'Pesetas don't make prizes!' – now the glamour clubs came calling. 'Ding dong!'

It was a time of glamour! Glamour clubs, glamour girls, Gary Glitter and glamorous rock!

Well, I may have been happy where I was, er, wherever it was at the time. But put yourself in my shoes. Who can resist the lure of a glamour club, hmm? Ho ho! Not yours truly!

The lure of 'Madame Fifi's Bawdy House', actually – where a slight misunderstanding with a man of the cloth led to a minor fracas (be fair! – it looked like a 'nightie' to me) all resulting in a bit of local scandal which hastened my departure to the Northwest to accept the poisoned chalice at Maine Road – marvellous!

Soon I was holding my first press conference as the new manager of Manchester City, then in free-fall in the old First Division. For many on the terraces, and in the directors' box, avoiding the drop was a physical impossibility. Speculation was rife in the press – could I do it? Was Ron up to the job?

'The word "can't" isn't in my dictionary!' I assured them – immediately getting myself off on the wrong foot with the Northern reporters unused to my Ponders Bar accent. I awoke the next day to the headlines 'The filth and the fury!' and a flurry of letters telling me that the word 'c**t' was actually on page 388 of the Collins Concise. Marvellous!

And yet, despite all my efforts and stout resistance, City continued in free-fall – completely invalidating Newton's law of motion⋆!

⋆ Newton's first law of motion. Something about an object moving and the forces what act upon it. In this case – yours truly – marvellous.

But, the confidence of youth, isn't it? If anyone could make a silk purse out of a sow's ear, it was Ron Manager. There's a knack to it – I'd once even made myself a lovely pair of slippers out of a couple of pig's ears. Beat that!

Even in the final minute of our last-ditch relegation struggle, I alone remained bullish and upbeat. As we conceded a pointless free-kick near the centre-circle, I rounded on my tormentors, taunting the vultures in the press box with my celebrated faux pas –

'If he scores from there, I'll eat my hat!'

– turning back to watch in horror as Bob Hail's feeble shot picked up pace from the wet pitch and rocketed into the corner of the net – completely invalidating Newton's second law of motion*. And sadly, having already eaten my hat after making a similar rash promise to the gentlemen of the press a couple of games earlier, I was forced to eat my slippers as we went down with all guns blazing. Marvellous!

I looked upon it as another blessing in disguise. How often our finest moments arrive cloaked in abject failure! It's all just part of life's glorious debacle, isn't it, hmm?

Call it destiny if you like, but some of us are just born ahead of our time. People often say I was born with an old head on young shoulders, which is perhaps why I was kept in the cupboard under the stairs until the rest of me caught up.

But new ideas are rarely accepted overnight and you

---

* A ball can't pick up pace off of wet turf – or if you want to be pedantic . . . $ke = 1/2\ mv^2$, marvellous!

can't make an omelette without treading on some toes. Connoisseurs of the beautiful game often point out that it was Ron who sowed the seeds of the Sky Blues' eventual return to the top flight. That's 'The Manager Method'* – marvellous!

★ 'Hoof, hoof, rush!'

CHAPTER ELEVEN

HAIR! ISN'T IT?

*'This is the dawning of the age of Aquarius
. . . ho ho . . . the age of Aquarius.'*

I don't get it, Ron.

It's a feeble 'arse joke', Joan.

ARRIVING at Maine Road for pre-season training, only to find my contract terminated by mutual agreement, did not bother me one whit! . . . Hang on a minute . . .

Joan, where's the dictionary?

Yes! Did it bother me? – not a sausage! In many ways I was pleased. I've never been one to brood, and as far as I was concerned, they could stick their rotten club! And despite the press clamouring for me to dish the dirt, I wasn't going to make any hasty remarks I might later regret. Ho ho! Unlike the wife! She shoots from the hip!

They'd get their quote all right – but first I wanted to chew things over. I'm a masticator! hmm?

If they wanted one off the cuff, they could ask Joan!

Ron, I'm looking for the dictionary, I've only got two hands.

Besides, 'lose some, draw some', isn't it? When the chips were down, I'd stuck my neck out – and ricked the bloomin' thing. But hey, life goes on! Isn't it?

I walked out through the gates of Maine Road, with my best foot forward, my chest out, and my head held high.

Confronted by the gaggle of bewildered newshounds hovering like vultures outside, I greeted them with urbane, insouciant nonchalance – they must have thought I was mad!

'Ron, have you lost it?' Cheeky pups!

I reassured them, 'Gentlemen, I've put it behind me.'

At which point it dawned on me that they were actually enquiring about my head – and to be fair, with chest out, foot forward and a ricked neck, the old noddle's bound to be set back a bit, hmm?

I remained dignified and aloof. Carefully choosing my words, I brushed the press aside with nothing more than a few terse remarks.

'Gentlemen, I have other fish to fry.'

Heartfelt words – it was my wedding anniversary and nothing was going to spoil the romantic candlelight dinner

I'd promised my beloved Joan. This was only a hiccup.

And besides, even as I spoke, I knew that, as sure as night follows day, Ron would be back – I'd left a brace of kippers in the dressing room and Joan would have bloomin' killed me!

But football directors are an impatient bunch, hmm? They want everything done yesterday*! Be fair, Rome wasn't built in a day, was it?

Joan, have you checked this out yet? I may be making a bit of a 'Charlie' of myself here.

After many years' experience on the managerial merry-go-round, you can take it from Ron Manager, no matter how much money you fling at a team, you can't knock down a coconut every time. In the end, it all comes down to one thing – desire, hmm? Isn't it? Without trying to pass the buck, let me put it bluntly – if the lads aren't up for it, you're 'poked'.

And so, slightly disillusioned and completely p*ked, I decided to concentrate on my side-line – my boutique. Jackets with two-foot lapels! Tank-tops! Kipper ties! Marvellous!

And before you start thinking that running a fashion boutique is only for pansies, this was the seventies – all us football faces were pansies of a sort in those days!

'Ron's Significant Strides' opened with great fanfare in early 1976. Well, not that great a fanfare actually – having

---

★ Kippers?

blown most of the promotional budget on hiring Bianca Jagger sitting astride a donkey, I could only afford a couple of trombonists and an old fellow with a kazoo.

But what a party we had that night – the Village People singing one of their bawdy classics over and over, as we danced till dawn – and I was a bit of a dandy in my day you know! And not just a nod in the direction of the latest fashion trends. When Ron took the floor, without wanting to sound a bit racy, it was the whole blooming caboodle*! Platform shoes with quarter-inch soles, a 'puffer fish' cravat (not a big seller – I've still got a couple of dozen of the bloomin' things under the bed – the kids love 'em!), bell-bottomed loon pants – which would subsequently feature Ron's innovative patented double-stitched crotch, a pair having split on me mid-air, as I performed one of my two-footed, splay-legged leaps, while dancing to Tina Charles. I didn't even notice at first – it was hardly the first time my crazy gyrations had inspired shouts of, 'Ron, yer nuts!' – but after a bewildering conversation with Bianca over what constituted a legitimate tackle, the penny dropped – she was talking b**l**ks, quite literally! – and with the Manager 'tackle' swinging ebulliently I was out of there like the clappers!

What a night! Hmm? 'Yessir, I can boogie . . .' Ho ho – and so could Ron Manager! What a dancer! I could bloomin' boogie – watusi, jive, pop, and only a long-standing metatarsal problem prevented me from 'wowing'

★ Abbrev**. – 'kit and caboodle'.
★★ Short for abbreviation.

the dance-floor with the mashed potato. The night seemed to go on forever! Demis Roussos bloomin' did! With the night's schedule completely out of whack, I eventually had to cancel a somewhat tearful St Winifred's School Choir, and slip them a few bob to slope off quietly. If I hadn't, Bernard Manning and his 'entourage' would have had my guts for garters – literally!

Heady times, wasn't it? Though still a football man through and through, I was now embracing the worlds of clubland and showbiz. And these were the days of big names and big personalities – sorry, BIG NAMES! BIG PERSONALITIES! Soccer's equivalent of the rat-pack!

Big Al, Big Mal, Big Val, Big Ron, Big Norm! Big fedoras, big Cohibas, big potatoes – every s**g*e one of 'em! I should know – I performed alongside them all in a Footie All-Stars Charity Performance of *Hair*.

And in those days people in the football world did have hair! Well, apart from old Bald Eagle obviously! Ho ho! Sorry, that's one of my 'funnies'. Hang on a minute . . .

Joan, note that down for one of my hilarious TV ad-libs.

Good call, Ron! You don't waste a cracker like that – not when you're up against such razor-sharp wits as Ray Stubbs and Bob Wilson.

Hmm? Where was I? Oh yes, *Hair*. Don't remember it? Go and ask your dad. What a cracking show! 'Theatrical Viagra' in those more innocent times before we needed it! – that Ms Kidman didn't invent it, you know.

Ho ho! All of us buck naked – except for Jim Smith, who retained his trademark flat cap in order to secure his flowing wig. Looking back I can scarcely believe my own audacity! I was a bit reticent at first, after seeing the West End cast. Us fellows can be a bit concerned about the size of our 'manhood' you know! and naturally feel a little uncomfortable when confronted by a stage full of over-endowed freaks. Be fair, most of them were probably pansies, but some had, you know, 'doodahs' bigger than my middle blooming toe! But though the idea of making my first appearance on the boards was somewhat daunting, the more often I saw the show, the more I was up for it! Could Ron throw off his inhibitions and let it all hang out? – hmm? – maybe they'd let me just poke it out a little bit.

What finally swung it for me was meeting the cast back-stage and being let into a little secret. And without breaking the code of the 'magic circle', all I can tell you is, it's an old thespian trick of the trade involving nothing more than a quick dunk of the doodah in a bowl of warm water before making your entrance! 'Medium Ron' marvellous!

Where was I? Oh yes. Make the most of your assets, hmm? It's a big world out there, marvellous! And a word to the unwary – don't boil 'em lads!

Ron Manager – thespian, isn't it? – Treading the boards with aplomb! And to great acclaim, I might add – Well, I just have – shrewd stuff! – us book-writers get paid by the word, you know!

Nonetheless . . .

Here, Joan, check if 'nonetheless' counts as three words, otherwise I'll just give it the old 'nevertheless'.

But *Hair*, wasn't it? The hippie musical. To be honest, none of us footie folk would have touched a hippie with a barge-pole – dirty, unkempt, sponging drop-outs, often four-eyed and possibly smelling of BO. But their 'chicks', hmm? Marvellous!

I'll never forget Moonsnowdrop – honking of patchouli oil, doe-eyed, splay-footed, chubby, a little unkempt perhaps, yet extravagantly buxom – but that's not what you noticed, just her natural radiance shining through like two great beacons!

Let's doff our caps to *Hair* – might be old hat nowadays – for Jim Smith it was 'old hat' in the seventies! Ho ho! Wait a minute –

Joan, save this under 'Ron's gems'.

– but racy blooming stuff for the times, wasn't it? Full-blown nudity on stage – didn't even have full-blown nudity at home in those days – don't bloomin' have half-blown . . .

Er, sorry Joan, take this out.

But it fired my imagination sufficiently to sink all my savings into opening a second boutique: 'The Emperor's New Clothes Shop' – only to be forced to cease trading by the Fraud Squad two days later, taking 'Ron's Significant Strides' down with it.

But without blowing my own trumpet, even if my first venture into the rag trade never made it to the King's Road, it still does roaring business mail-order from Scunthorpe – mainly thanks to John Barnes, I believe!

The seventies? What times to be a young man in his prime, hmm? Marvellous!

But all things come to an end, and that same year, as I sadly shut the shutters and sat in the shop listening to the radio as Malcolm Allison's Palace team broke Chelsea hearts on Valentine's Day, I knew I had to get back into football. And though it may have been a quarter of a century ago*, it seems like only yesterday** that I was marching back into top-level management, confidently telling the press that this time I was there for the long haul. Ron Manager was no fly-by-night – literally!

'Judge me in three years' time,' I announced as I strolled purposefully through the gates at Stamford Bridge. Which was all a bit embarrassing, actually, I'd set out for Fulham – who eventually showed me the door themselves three days later. It's hardly worth going into all the details here, but, you know, the same old story isn't it? A sorry tale of meagre resources, a 'sticky patch' er, the physio's wife – you know the kind of thing, hmm? Marvellous!

And so, with the press hot on my heels, I left hot-foot for that hotbed of soccer – Bonnie Scotland! Bloody freezing! Without so much as a backward glance, I caught

---

★ Approximately.
★★ Wednesday.

the first sleeper out of King's Cross – thumbing my nose at the angry posse arriving belatedly at platform ten, to the howl of the steam whistle, and the 'whump' and 'whoof' of pumping pistons, as the train chugged out of the station. Ho ho! You've got to get up early to catch Ron Manager – and they bloomin' nearly did!

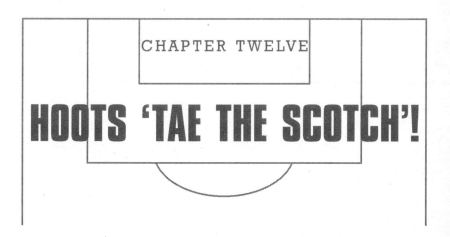

CHAPTER TWELVE

HOOTS 'TAE THE SCOTCH'!

Scotch football? Hoots! Where's your trousers?
Isn't it? Marvellous!

LET'S have a look at how the Scotch have contributed to football . . .

Ron, they won't pay you for this page.

Eh? But it's one of my 'funnies'! All right . . . hang on . . .

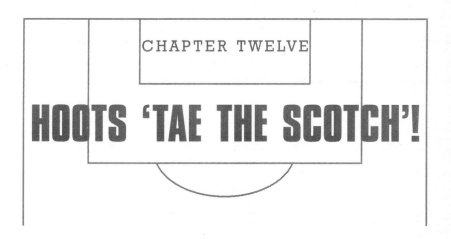

CHAPTER TWELVE

HOOTS 'TAE THE SCOTCH'!

'Awa' wi' ye . . . Ye wee cowrin' tim'rous beasties!'

THE Scotch! Marvellous, isn't it? Bravehearts, aren't they? Well, to be fair, the diet's not for the lily-livered! Hmm? But what an influence this tiny backward nation has had on the beautiful game. From their dourly efficient, humourless managers all the way down to those jinky jocks – the little fellows you often used to find doing their bandy-legged thing up and down the wing. Bit like the Irish, actually, you know, Bestie, er, Giggsy . . .

Let's celebrate the Celtic nations! Ladies and gentlemen, let's drink a toast to the Scotch and the Irish!

Ron, you forgot the Welsh.

Ho ho! Of course! As we raise our glasses, make sure you keep an eye on your handbags, ladies! Thieving b*gg**s the Taffs, aren't they?

The Celts, hmm? Though lacking the reliability and self-control of us Englishmen – turning up for games a little worse for wear, or letting the side down in a mystifying rush of blood – in many ways, they're our closest living relatives. And besides, take the likes of Bestie! Always capable of turning a match with a moment of magical spontaneity, when he was on fire he could win games single-handedly!

Yet even George couldn't hold a candle to Calum Iain MacFhearghais – there was the archetypal fiery Scot. Five minutes before kick-off* he would burst into the dressing room, literally! Ruddy and apoplectic, a fish supper tucked under his armpit, a wee dram clutched in bony fingers, he'd brush past us, eyes staring madly under his wild ginger mane, greeting us warmly in his native Scotch.

'Oot ma road, ahm bustin!'

But when the whistle blew and the chips were down, Calum 'wis the wee** boy!' Or was he the Big Yin? Three down on aggregate in the quarter-final second leg, reduced to ten men, his reaction was spontaneous. Cometh the hour, er, combusteth the man – leaving nothing but a small patch of scorched earth and a pair of smouldering boots. Enduring image, hmm?

Down to nine men, we took a terrible hammering. Marvellous! We all took it quite calmly, except perhaps for Bob Pipe who from that day on would eat nothing but nuts and berries, and stopping people in the street, would

---

* 2.55 pm – even in Scotland.
** Scotch for small. Always makes me laugh. Does it you, hmm?

fix them with a glassy stare, and tell them, 'Every day's my quarter-final second leg these days!'

Eventually Bob pulled himself together and went off and joined the Moonies.

But Scotchmen, hmm? You ask the man in the street the first thing that springs to mind about the Scotch – a few pints of 'heavy', a Mars bar in the deep-fat fryer and a chip on the shoulder! And maybe that's why, as the modern game places ever more emphasis on diet and physical fitness, this proud, traditionally unhealthy and ultimately doomed nation has fallen by the wayside. Be fair, the body beautiful? The Jocks? Hmm? Ho ho! Marvellous!

But just because the vast majority of this fiercely independent race of alcoholic bigots seems to be still stuck in the dark ages, let's not tar them all with the same brush. Some of my best friends are Scotch – I even speak a 'wee' bit of the lingo, er, 'maself'.

'An' a big hello tae wee Jeannie frae Paisley!' 'How's yer erse?' 'Yer maw's a man!' – marvellous!

And the much-perceived image of a country still obsessed with the auld enemy, mutton pies and the Battle of the Boyne is way off the mark.

I've always had a deep affinity for our Caledonian cousins. Not mine, mind you – a more tight-fisted, miserable bunch of shites you'd never wish to meet. I always had a soft spot for my grandmother, though – and there was a ferociously religious woman! She often had two religions on the go at once – returning home from putting a fatwa on the head of the local orange lodge, to while away her evening sticking pins in her 'wee' Plasticene effigy of the Pope.

101

Fair game! They're harmless folk! But when some arrogant jock tries to tell you that they invented football? It makes the blood run wild! Take it from Ron, he's talking guff! It was invented here in England – centuries ago, by a bunch of ale-swilling louts punting an inflated pig's bladder through the streets of a picturesque little village. Enduring image, isn't it? Yet not such a far cry from the beautiful game we know today, hmm?

Soccer! It's the great English invention, uniting nations in peace and harmony! Don't listen to their guff! The Scots think they've invented everything – and it's all guff!

The light bulb? Television? Bloomin' unthinkable, isn't it?

Golf, perhaps, the noble art of whacking a little ball around with a stick, but football? Hmm? Not likely! If a Scotsman got hold of a pig's bladder, he'd probably stuff it with oats and sing songs to it! Hang on! – or he'd attach a bit of plumbing to it, and try to squeeze a tune out of it with his armpit! (Ho ho! I've got my witty hat pulled down tight here, eh?)

But still we retain this obsession with Scotch managers. What baleful influence does this bandy-legged ginger race hold over the beautiful game? – and before anyone accuses me of being racist, let me tell you some of my best friends are 'sweaties' – Mrs Manager's got a bit of Scotch in her – probably even as I speak! We even spent some of our courting days in Bonnie Scotland – Joan coyly suggesting a dirty weekend at her aunt Jeannie's caravan in Govan! Ho ho! That saucy look – hmm?

'But Ron, remember you'll have to get off at Paisley!'

If only I'd known it was a colloquialism – bloomin' long walk, I was cream-crackered! – easy to get hold of the wrong end of the stick, isn't it?

Now they're trying to bring Rangers and Celtic down here, and according to Rangers' chairman, David Murray, they are 'all singing from the same hymn-sheet'. Ho ho! Well it might put the willies up the Fenians in the Nationwide! But be fair, all that sectarianism? It's just a lot of harmless piffle*, isn't it? It puts bums on seats, literally. The auld alliance isn't it? Let's face it, without Rangers, Celtic would be like blooming Hibs!

Do they really think they're going to come down south and devalue our glorious Premiership with their kick-in-the-park-style football, and pollute our 'beautiful game' with their insane sectarian antics? Relish the tussle? Re-daub the wattle! Re-build the wall!

Does anyone outside Mrs Manager and her beetle drive want to see Mel Gibson and his Caledonian cronies baring their arses? Let Ron give you it straight – 'Bah!'

Ho ho! That's the Scotch! Marvellous! Yet though it would be easy to dismiss them as nothing but a bunch of miserable wasters, they've contributed a couple of decent players, I suppose.

So let's celebrate the Scotch! Let's have a 'wee skug' at the Jocks who're still tearing it up in the modern game today. In descending order . . .

No. 5: Bertie Vogts! Ho ho! Only joking! He's a German!

No. 5: Graeme Souness – scared of no man! Went to

---

* Guff.

Turkey and planted a Galatasaray flag in the middle of the Fenerbahce pitch. Cold-blooded determination personified! – softly spoken, but not in that twitchy vicious whispering sort of way normally associated with the traditional Scotch psychopath! Though to be fair you wouldn't want Graeme as your enemy – not unless you want to get a flagpole poked impudently into your centre circle! Marvellous!

No. 4: 'Wee' Gordon Strachan. He has his ups and downs but he's been irrepressible latterly – like a little Scotch terrier, literally! Always up for the challenge – vertically! And for the full ninety minutes, virtually. Literally no one covers more distance laterally than Gordon does vertically. Will he succeed in his hilarious pursuit of mid-table mediocrity? Life's a lottery – literally!

But according to others in the upper echelons of the beautiful game, er, wee Gordon's the 'Scotchman's Scotchman' – the Cahoochy man! Ho ho, get this – 'The sairer he faws the mair he stoats!' Great stuff! Told you I spoke the lingo! 'Och aye the noo, Jimmy!'

No. 3: George Graham. Can a man not be linked with a top managerial position these days without having to share the headlines with this dour disciplinarian? hmm?

No. 2: Sir Alex Ferguson – scared of no man! Called Ken Bates Chairman Mao! Prowling the touchline at Old Trafford – chewing furiously! As inscrutable as Fu Manchu! Hmm? Like, er, Chu Manchu – builds a team in his own image, hmm? The whistle blows, the red mist descends – marvellous!

No. 1: Kylie Minogue. Sorry, thought she actually was

Scotch – but let me take this opportunity to 'scotch' all those rumours about myself getting a little over-familiar with the diminutive sex-bomb when celebrating our joint fifth place in that charity penalty shoot-out.

Despite the financial inducements offered to me by my publishers for some racy gossip – hoping to 'bump up' the serialisation rights for the gutter press – all I am prepared to say is – yes, Kylie does have a soft spot for me! But Ron Manager doesn't 'kiss 'n' tell' – I could never stoop so low! – mum's the word, isn't it? Marvellous! And say what you like, Kylie might not be able to hit a coo's erse wi' a banjo, but she's certainly got a 'flair for dancin'' – and a 'behind' you can't shake a stick at! Marvellous!

Ho ho! That should get 'em! . . . I'll be up in a second, Joan. Bung on the Teasmade!

CHAPTER THIRTEEN

PLAYBOYS OF THE KING'S ROAD

'Football's rubbish now – maybe they was boozing, gambling womanisers in the seventies, but they was Chelsea through and through!'

'Ho ho! And so was we, Norm! So was we!'

SEVENTY-SIX, wasn't it? hmm? Punk rock not yet in its pomp – but furious pogo-ing to 'Knees Up Mother Brown' down at the Bridge! While London sizzled in a heat wave, 'Soccer's Siamese twins', Ron Manager and Big Norm, thundered down the King's Road, through a human sea of fishnet stockings, safety-pins and rivers of 'gob' rolling turgidly down the gutters – marvellous! – headed for Chelsea FC in the back of Norm's roller. We'd come a long way from Fulham! And though my trusty number two had spent his teenage years hurling abuse on the terraces, this was my first encounter with the playboys of Stamford Bridge – one of the many 'homes' of football.

There's not many of us top footballing faces who haven't spent some time in the revolving doors at Chelsea – dizzy days on the managerial merry-go-round, isn't it, hmm? Fortunately within the hour we had been rescued by one of those Chelsea Pensioner fellows – not Ken Bates! Ho ho! Get it?

Ron, we might have to take that out.

And so, tottering and bilious, we were escorted to the reception desk by a dead ringer for Ol' Captain Birdseye, to take up our new positions – myself, Ron Manager, in the then newly invented position of director of football and Big Norm as trainee groundsman – 'Have roller will travel', isn't it? – I'll bet the groundsman at Fulham hadn't even missed it!

What does a director of football do, hmm? Ho ho! See my next chapter – What a director of football actually does!

Ron, they won't let you have another 'comedy' page.

Eh? Humourless bunch! Oh well, let's plug on . . .

Director of football, isn't it? Marvellous! At last, a chance to influence a team away from the pressure of the dugout, kept at arm's length from the mundane day-to-day drudgery of the first team. It made for a refreshing change from the boiling emotions of the touchline – though eventually, after a few weeks mooching around listening to Big Norm's constant insane gibbering rantings, I cajoled and pleaded to be given a more hands-on role. And so, although it meant me accepting a considerable drop in salary, they grudgingly handed me the keys to the canteen, where I forged the dietary revolution which possibly single-handedly sowed the seeds of Chelsea's revival as the team of the new millennium!

Glenn Hoddle's crackers! Hmm? We've all heard how this most mystical of managers had to bring his own biscuits with him when he took over at Chelsea, but I doubt that even Glenn knows that he was only following in the footsteps of Ron Manager. As so often before I had already been there, done that – stood in it, and trodden it all round the room on the sole of my shoe – marvellous!

Yes, as in so many walks of life, it's the small details that make the difference – and the sight of my Hob-Nobs immediately raised morale at the club, much as they had in the dressing room at Fulham. When I first arrived, the high rollers of west London were used to tucking into ice-cream and rabbit-shaped jelly! Don't worry! I soon knocked that on the head. People used to tell me, 'Ron, you broke the mould!' – ho ho! That was Ron Manager in his pomp! I sat on it actually.

Nowadays the Italian revolution's well underway at the Bridge. Claudio Ranieri's Garibaldis are now the flavour of the month. He's certainly overturned everyone's initial misgivings about employing a manager who had hardly mastered the lingo! – Claudio's gesticulations speak louder than words – well, not literally, obviously, that would be stupid – unless he slapped himself about a bit, I suppose.

Don't expect Ron Manager to come over all xenophobic here – the cosmopolitan set-up at Chelsea's fine! Whether it's wops, spics, frogs, turds or the Hun, there's no language barrier in football. When I arrived at Hartlepool with my broad Potter's End accent I made myself understood with an extravagant display of body language, winks, half-remembered semaphore, and hastily scribbled notes on the back of a cigarette packet. Football's a universal language! Eager to pass on my experience, I met Claudio for dinner up at 'Papa Ken's' Trattoria in Chelsea Village – food like mamma used to make! Ho ho! Not like my 'mamma', I hope! (Sorry mum!)

And this son of an Italian butcher has come a long way and he knows his bloomin' onions! Mindful of the press reports of his lack of English, I've plumped for his mother tongue – so he's plumped for mine! What did we talk about? Bloomin' football, of course. Almost immediately we were locked into a deep tactical discussion – manager to Manager, and he's much more fluent than he lets on!

'. . . Er, so, Claudio him reckon *catenaccio* eez old hat, hmm?'

Ho ho! His swarthy little face has lit up! An insouciant look as he measures his words, 'F**k off c*nker-bolloc*s!'

Reckon little Dennis Wise has been having some fun again, hmm? I had to laugh.

But if you want to compete on the European circuit you've got to learn the lingoes, isn't it? Hats off to the multi-lingual chancers of the modern game!

Be fair, how many of us pick up a new language overnight, hmm? But when Johnny Foreigner's just getting to grips with the Queen's English – ho ho! – gives you a bit of a chuckle, doesn't it? No offence, but they do sound, you know, a bit 'daft' – well, all right, 'thick'. It always makes me laugh. Marvellous!

But they certainly respect Claudio Ranieri at the Bridge, and here in relaxed surroundings he's at his most effusive. Luigi the waiter hovering attentively ho ho – he's born and bred in SW6, can't speak a word of Italian! – 'No problema!' Claudio takes charge. A few minutes of wild gesticulation secures us a couple of beers, a jug of popcorn and a small leather hat. Marvellous!

It's all a far cry from my own time with the mighty Blues. Back in the dark days before football visionary Ken Bates had transformed the club into a mighty multinational empire. There's certainly been some changes down at Stamford Bridge. They weren't always so well catered for at the Bates Motel! And although reluctant to hand in my notice, with the coming of the great man, I had little choice but to tender my resignation. The night of the blunt knives, wasn't it, hmm?

But no hard feelings! The club was in need of a new broom, and I knew that even Ron would eventually be swept aside. And though widely quoted at the time as laconically saying, 'If it ain't broke, what's your beef?' I actually put one over you there, Ken! – I've still got the old broom in my garden shed and if you don't sweep too vigorously, it's just as effective as it was back then! Marvellous.

But for all the haute cuisine and function rooms, Stamford Bridge nowadays is a shadow of its former self.

What happened to the atmosphere at football? Without wanting to propose a return to the bad old days of hooliganism, I do sometimes wonder – have we thrown the baby out with the bath water, hmm?

For a football team, a passionate crowd is their twelfth man. And didn't the fans used to turn the air blue at Chelsea, hmm? And yet nowadays they get flung out of the ground if they so much as hurl abuse or urinate! – Be fair, it's not really football till it all kicks off, hmm?

And I sometimes feel a pang of guilt that I may have inadvertently triggered the decline of this once proud club. Not that anyone at Chelsea had seemed to pay me a blind bit of notice at the time!

Yet running into Chopper Harris recently, I was amazed to hear him tell me how I had transformed his whole attitude to life and made him a changed man. Yes it was yours truly, Ron Manager, who had set him on his road to Damascus. Well blow me! I was made up. I insisted on buying him a drink. But while returning from the bar, masterfully balancing a pint in each hand, Joan bringing up the rear meekly clutching her Babycham, I was suddenly taken out with a scything lunge – and looked up in time to see that familiar cheeky grin – before the blue mist again descended, and he stamped on my face! That was Chopper – still that same old apple-cheeked boy. Marvellous.

And yet, to be fair, I must admit that during my time among the playboys of the King's Road, I had not always gazed on him so fondly. Whenever he took the field I couldn't help but notice the twinkle in Joan's eye, as she looked him up and down with a curious expression that hitherto she had reserved only for myself and Dino. And although to the best of my knowledge her strange fascination with the rugged Chelsea hardman was entirely innocent, I knew intuitively that her passion for me was fading. The seven-year itch isn't it? hmm?

Here, Joan! What happened to my Ruud Gullit wig?

Ron, you used to complain that it was hot and itchy, and it made your eczema flare up – and you ate it after one of your stupid predictions.

Oh. Where was I? Oh yes, the sensational seventies wasn't it? Maybe as I was spending too much time away from Joan, I had the notion that we might be drifting apart.

It's that sort of sixth sense that all of us top managers have. On nights out with the girls she would be dolled up to the nines – a vision in lipstick, powder and paint – while our romantic evenings at home would be spent with a cigarette dangling from her lower lip, breaking wind with reckless abandon as if completely unconcerned that she might 'follow through'. Bloomin' marvellous, isn't it?

My suspicions were raised further one night when Joan and myself were dining out with Michael Winner in a candle-lit bistro in Covent Garden – Joan bawling with laughter at every one of his 'funnies', while my own shafts of wit were greeted with a stony silence and a look of disdain as if I had made a bad smell – which, coincidentally, I just have.

Now, with my new celebrity status in soccer circles, I

found myself spending more time in the company of my football family. Even without my own sudden interest in the female form, my relationship with Joan had become strained. Our home life had become a drudge. The love-boat we had paddled all the way from bonny Italee lay upturned on the shore, battered and barnacled*. My marriage to Joan was on the rocks – women are fickle creatures, hmm? – and the stressful life of a 'Director of Football' – twenty-five hours a day, eight days a week – well, it's bound to take its toll on any relationship. Mrs Manager and myself had become like two ships in the night, occasionally bumping together in the wee hours – alarm bells ringing as *The* SS *Joan* came looming out of the darkness, bearing down on *The Good Ship Manager* as it hastily turned astern, and nearly knocking my blooming barnacles** off!

---

* Covered in those crustaceans that fasten themselves to the bottom of old boats.
** Small limpet, see chapter eight.

CHAPTER FOURTEEN

ALONE AGAIN, NATURALLY

'Women are from Venus? Ho ho!
Well f**k my old boots . . .'

WHENEVER people ask who was responsible for the breakdown of my marriage, Ron Manager has never passed the buck. Without being over-analytical about what had gone wrong with our relationship, I think it's fair to say that basically Joan had just got the right hump with me! And when she opened her newspaper on the morning of our tenth wedding anniversary to that tabloid photo-shoot of me doing 'the Hustle' with Clodagh Rodgers it was the straw that broke the camel's back.

But that's life in the public eye, isn't it, hmm? I wouldn't mind, but I was only offered the bloomin' job as a last-minute replacement for future England stand-in supremo Peter Taylor whose missus got wind of it, and pulled him out at the last minute! But at least he managed to win her round and patch things up. Humour! Isn't it? That was Peter Taylor's *forte*. Ho ho! 'Mr Grimsdale . . . Mr Grimsdaaale . . .'

Norman Wisdom in his pomp! Marvellous!

Ho ho! Mrs Taylor couldn't be angry with Peter for long. But it doesn't work for us all, hmm? Unfortunately Joan remained cold and aloof, and sat stony-faced as I attempted to cajole her back into some semblance of affection for me with my endless variations on why the chicken had crossed the road. Draw some, lose some, hmm?

But even if Joan no longer had a laugh left in her, it's funny how what works with the fairer sex, often works in football. And just as Peter's famous Norman Wisdom impersonations helped to smooth things over with the wife, so they helped him build team spirit and relieve the tension in the dressing room. Show me an England team that hasn't had its fair share of clowns over the years. And yes, a sense of humour is always a big hit with the ladies, I can tell you. Women are just like men in many ways, and, er, in others they're not.

Devastated by Joan packing her bags, but fully understanding her position – be fair, how can anyone sustain a relationship never knowing where your better half's going to be from one minute to the next? It would drive even a normal woman barmy. So I watched impotently, as the best woman I'd ever known – the mother of my children, the co-signatory on my chequebook, my heart, my soul, my bloomin' everything – effed off with some effing ponce from her local effing leisure centre. In fucking Epping!

F*****g marvellous! Isn't it?

I was gutted!

So every Saturday night at eight o'clock sharp, it was down to the Purple Pussycat. Ron Manager! In his pomp! Once again footloose and fancy-free. Ho ho! Marvellous!

Some of you will be a little surprised at the thought of Ron Manager, 'football man', prancing about on the dance-floor like er, a 'pansy', I suppose, but in truth there's always been plenty of crossovers between the world of dance and the beautiful game. Think about it! You'll see plenty of parallels. We're all hoofers, aren't we? Jinky footwork, silky skills, silky, er, outfits. I was always a 'bit of a mover' – well, I had to be! hmm?

And it works both ways. From the hard-hitting stage show *Zigger-Zagger* to that hard-hitting Ben Elton thing that folded recently, the dancing game has always taken inspiration from football. Not long ago, I accompanied Big Norm to a ballet based on Scotchman Archie Gemmill's wonder goal against Brazil! And as we shared a bucket of popcorn, the memories came flooding back, of an unforgettable European Cup tie pitted against Dynamo Kiev. Oddly enough, I'm as popular in Kiev as Norman Wisdom is in Albania. There even used to be a fifty-foot-high stone effigy of me there, until a night of high jinks with a coach party of Taliban tourists got a little out of hand. But in the away leg of our match in the Ukraine, I hit a rich seam of form. I was playing out of my skin – literally! – setting off on wave after wave of mazy dribbles, in my then little-imitated but utterly effective style – both elbows tucked in, keeping a low centre of gravity, haring around with long athletic strides, with the ball seemingly glued to my feet as I weaved through their entire defence at breakneck speed. In a word, I played an absolute blinder! Carried off shoulder-high by my team-mates – with almost an hour left to play!

And there was more to come. At a civic reception in our honour after the game, a local dance troupe suddenly announced a tribute and – blow me! – one of those little Cossack dancers came belting on to the stage and, with a large pom-pom tied to one of his boots, proceeded to give a visually dazzling and stunningly accurate depiction of my inadvertent own goal which had clinched the tie for Kiev. Marvellous! Ron Manager in full flow – in his pomp!

But let's return to the action. Follow me back to the Purple Pussycat, quite a favourite haunt for us football folk in those days. How many famous footie names from today cut their teeth cutting a rug under the famous mirror ball, before getting them knocked out for looking at one of the bouncers in a 'funny way', hmm?

Suddenly the world of showbiz met the world of football – face-to-face, head-to-head, back-to-back and belly-to-belly. Neither would ever be the same again. Marvellous!

What a time to be free and single and disengaged! Even on a bit of a slow night, the club would be literally heaving with 'crumpet' – as we used to call it in those heady days. Ho ho! As I tripped the light fantastic, I remember thinking to myself, if only Joan could see Ron 'cods-in-bed'* Manager now!

---

* I've just been told this alludes to the poor quality of our sex-life – thanks a bunch, Joan!

Bolero!
... marvellous...
hmm, isn't it?

The spellbinding
Erica Roe... look
at the jugs on that!

Training. Don't call Ron Manager a tracksuit manager... but note loosened tie.

The gaffer's gaffer takes charge of a gruelling coaching session. Mind your 'bovrils' Ron.

Get a load of my titfers! A modern manager needs to wear a bewildering array of hats... metaphorically of course. But it's not all hard graft, take a look at the next page...

Above: ... pretending to guide in a DC-10 during a lighter moment in training.

Below: 'Who are you calling a divot?' Having a laugh with somebody. Marvellous.

Above: Whoops! The old Cup proves as elusive as ever. Doesn't it?

Below: 'Who can't manage a pi*s up in a brewery?'

Above: Gas.

Below: 'Who can't manage a p*ss...?'

... In denial...

... In de Amazon...

But it wasn't all one-way traffic. There was hardly a night I wasn't mown down in the street through my own stupidity – ho ho! – no, really.

But what I meant was, there was plenty of competition for the ladies as well. I remember Peter Taylor, cap at a stupid angle, trousers at half-mast, looking on forlornly, having narrowly failed to pull one of Pan's People. His famed 'Mr Grimsdaale!' dying on his lips as he watched her disappear into the night with a little fellow who'd convinced her he was Charlie Drake. '*Touché*!' Isn't it? Marvellous!

Big Names! Malcolm Allison came strolling in one night – trademark big Cohiba cigar, big fedora and a dolly-bird on each arm. Big Mal, wasn't it? He's only pulled a couple of 'go-go' dancers from *Godspell*! Big bazookas! Everything was big about Mal!

We've all tried to pounce on the talent, but Big Mal's 'givin' it all that' as 'El Tel' used to put it, the rest of us can't get a blooming word in edgeways. Your ladies love a fellow who can make them laugh, hmm?

'When's a biscuit tin like a fountain?'

'Hee hee, stop it . . . Stop it Mal, I can't breathe.'

'When it's a square tin!'

'Ah ha ha! Oh Mal, you're priceless!'

The rest of us are all watching glumly on the sidelines. But all that bubbly, hmm? We're all human, eh? Even Big Mal's got to slope off for a leak eventually. Cometh the hour, goeth the man! heh heh! – marvellous.

And – bingo! – I've steamed straight in with my impersonation of sixties funnyman Freddie 'Parrot-face' Davies.

'Thrrrrrrrrrrp . . . isn't it?'

The girls are lapping it up! Swaying backwards and for-wards in doe-eyed rapture.

'. . . Thentimental thongth . . . thentimental mel–oh–dees . . .' Ho ho! – got 'em!

But blow me! – here comes Jim Smith doing his 'funny walk' – Old Bald Eagle's trying to trump me by doing his Max Wall routine – very poor! The girls are nonplussed, it looks like I've cracked it, but . . .

'Eeeeeeeeeeeeeeh!'

Suddenly everyone turns round – it's Big Ron Atkinson, hauling his sheepskin coat behind him on a bit of string!

'Schnorbitz! Heel boy!

Eeeeeeeeeeeeeeh!'

And Big Ron's 'bang-on' 'Bernie Winters' has bagged him the bloomin' crumpet! Marvellous!

Great days, hmm? That was the seventies. Punk rock! stuff the Jubilee! The filth and the fury! Street parties! Trestle tables! The bunting and the bubbly, isn't it?

Victory in Europe! Hitler defeated! Lemonade and sponge cake for the kiddies, and lashings of warm ale and fisticuffs for the adults! 'Oops upside your head!' Dancing in the streets! The watusi! The hully-gully! The mashed potato! Couples surreptitiously shuffling off down the alley. Ho ho! What are they up to, hmm? We were all at it. Marvellous. 'How's your father?', isn't it?

''E's off with that bus conductress, mum!' Great stuff! We Brits love a street party – the bubbly and the bunting, isn't it? Not to mention Bubbly Bunty! No, I shouldn't really – but what the heck, it was a long time ago! Jubilee day! Ron Manager in his pomp – firing on all cylinders!

Surreptitiously shuffling off down the alley with Bunty, almost on the stroke of midnight. Ho ho! Marvellous! Cometh the hour, cometh the man!

'Sorry, Bunty, it's never happened before.'

But next morning, it was business as usual for the tiresome workaholic Ron Manager – a leaky defence, a goalie who'd lost his bottle, a lack of penetration up front . . . (er, sorry again, Bunty) – I had work to do! And after a few 'hairs of the dog', a couple of 'liveners', and a couple of 'stiffeners', I was back wheeling and dealing in the transfer market with renewed gusto.

As a nation nursed its collective hangover, I was back in harness doing what I did best. Ho ho! – I couldn't rest on my 'laurels'. And after a flurry of phone calls, come close of play I had managed to replace my back four.

It was only when I came to my senses a few days later that I realised I had inadvertently signed the Sex Pistols – marvellous.

But heady carefree times, wasn't it? We mixed work with pleasure. It was all so much more relaxed in those less image-conscious days, wasn't it? I doubt there's many chairmen in today's Premiership would relish the thought of their managers roaming around the West End in the company of gangsters, gamblers and showgirls, lest the tabloids got hold of it and splashed their lurid tales of excess all over the Sunday papers.

Yet looking back, I suppose some of the chaps then running the West End clubs were 'connected'. Some certainly did hang around with known hoodlums, but we footie folk treated it all as a bit of a laugh.

Having said that, let me tell you a horse's head in the bed does ruin your night, even if it's a joke. And if Big Ron Atkinson's reading this, and I know he will be, I haven't forgotten, and neither has Mrs Manager – at a stroke writing off my paisley pyjamas, the candlewick bedspread and the tenner she had on Lucky Boy in the 2.30 at Kempton! . . . er, heady days.

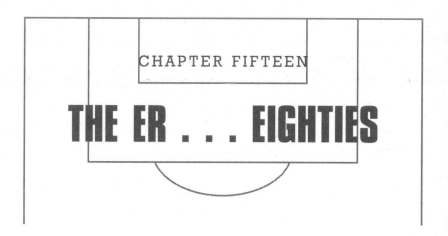

CHAPTER FIFTEEN

THE ER . . . EIGHTIES

'It's a simple game, you hoof it upfield and hopefully it bobbles in front of one of your players who can thump it into the net. One–all! . . . Marvellous!'

THATCHER'S Britain! The lady's not for turning! Shoulder pads! *Dallas*! Torville and Dean! Who shot JR? Ho ho! It wasn't bloomin' me! – street riots and New Romantics! It was all a far cry from those idyllic childhood days in Burnt End. It seemed the world I'd known was coming apart at the seams – the whole fabric of society was unravelling like a moth-eaten old jumper snagged on a rusty nail. This is great stuff, eh?

Now reconciled with Joan, who after a string of failed relationships had finally realised the error of her ways – be fair, there was no one who could ever replace her Ron! How could she have ever been so foolish? What blind naivety had led her to believe for one second . . .

Ron, put a sock in it, or you can get someone else to do your bloody proofreading.

Er, right ho! Now reconciled with Joan, I felt that after years of devoting myself to my career, it was time to put my family first, spend some time with my wife and get to know my son. Ferenc was now approaching his teens, and I was painfully aware that I had missed watching him grow up. That's life at the top for you! To be successful requires drive, ambition and total commitment. It's a full-time job. To be honest, I didn't actually recall that we had a son.

Yet suddenly, for the first time in my life, I found myself disenchanted with football. Disillusioned by the beautiful game which had bewitched, bothered, bewildered and eluded me for half a century*. It was as if something inside had died leaving only an empty husk of bitter memories of a love that used to be. And on top of that, to be fair, I was a bit buggered and could no longer be arsed.

After a few seasons striving, with little success, to steer once-mighty Brentford to mid-table mediocrity, things had taken a downward turn. Results had been going against us for some years, and I finally took the big decision. Although I had sworn I would never turn my back on the club, I bid farewell to the team I loved and I walked out on football – with no idea of where I was headed. In truth, it was possibly the most difficult thing

---

★ Approximately.

I'd ever done. You don't believe me? You bloomin' try it!

I'll never forget Mrs Manager's words as I arrived glumly on the doorstep . . .

'Ron, you stupid lump, why are you walking backwards?'

Yet although I had decided to put the beautiful game behind me and spend more time with my family, I hadn't reckoned on my doughty wife Joan. She wasn't having her Ron moping round the house while her and Ferenc were trying to watch Richard and Judy! Unused to seeing me so completely deflated, it was all hands to the pump – and I soon came bouncing back!

Be fair, I've always stood by my decisions and taken full responsibility for my actions. So what was the cause of this uncharacteristic U-turn? Blame the wife!

Joan had recently struck up a close friendship with one of the directors at Maine Road and with inside knowledge of an upcoming vacancy, after much humming and hawing – quite literally! – she decided to hurl my hat into the ring.

Hoopla! – as they say on the Continent. Or to put it in plain English – marvellous! And before you could say 'Walter Winterbottom', I once more found myself thrashing about frantically in the managerial melting-pot.

It was the same old story. The archetypal yo-yo club, isn't it? Soaring imperiously back into the top flight, only to find themselves out of their depth, struggling frantically for survival.

'Help!' they've bloomin' shouted, 'where's Ron?'

'Don't worry lads!' I've said, 'I'm back!'

Exciting stuff, hmm? Well you get the gist, anyway. But if they were looking for a 'quick fix' they could forget it. I demanded time to turn their fortunes around. So once again I found myself accepting the poisoned chalice at Manchester City, spending another £12 million as I haughtily took them back down to the old Second Division, only to be 'shafted'*and find myself unceremoniously dumped back on the top of the managerial scrapheap.

I'd had enough. This time Ron Manager had had it up to here**!

I dusted myself off and returned home, now determined to spend more time with my family. Not if good old Joan and Ferenc could help it! The minute I walked through the door, they could see I had been let down. Once more it was 'all hands to the pump' – and this time with such vigour, I came back with a bang!

And for reasons incomprehensible outside the crazy world of football, I made a swift return to the City hot seat, and was welcomed as their prodigal son – as I took them down for a third time! But it's a funny old game, isn't it?

Strangely, in the topsy-turvy world of football management, my star was now in the ascendant. As the life of a football manager became increasingly more like a game of musical chairs, my willingness to leap into a hot seat – still warm from the previous incumbent – was now much sought after. And if there was one place you never suffered a cold

---

✶ Done up like a kipper.
✶✶ About up to there.

126

'behind' it was the, er, 'White-Hot' Lane – 'Hart-seat'.

In football circles, I was regarded as a maverick – a loose cannon! – but I got results. And if anyone needed a ro*ket up the arse it was the under-achieving football connoisseurs of N17. The call went out for Ron.

Cometh the hour, cometh the man! Isn't it? hmm? But after three frustrating days in north London, I'd had enough. My terse remarks, then widely reported in the press, certainly raised a few eyebrows, but I was never one to mince my words.

'There used to be a football club over there, hmm?'

'Ron, it's over there.'

'Eh? How did I miss it?'

And by then the job had gone, so I, er, wenteth.

Suddenly I found myself in football limbo.

Now I needed a new challenge. It was time to spread my wings. It's a big world out there, isn't it and the beautiful game is the same beautiful game the world over – even if some of the supporters might be a little more attractive in other countries.

It was time to broaden my horizons. Football's a common language – not '!@*!*#!!' – ho ho! one of my 'funnies' – no, I mean football knows no boundaries. And Ron Manager was the last of the pioneers. Marvellous! It's a big world out there! So pinning Joan's fox-tail stole to the back of my Davy Crockett hat, I headed west and across the Severn Toll Bridge into Wales! *Cymru am Byth!*★ isn't it, eh?

★ That'll be ten pounds Boyo or the cottage gets it!

Regarded with a mixture of fear and envy by the villagers of Cardiff, many of whom had probably never seen an Englishman before, I shook my head in wry amusement as this proud race, untouched by modern civilisation, gazed awestruck at my modern-day 'trappings' before excitedly making off with my wristwatch, suitcase and shoes. I knew immediately I was going to be treated as one of their own.

'*Iechyd da pob Cymro – twll tin pob Sais*!' Hmm? Isn't it? '*Ardderchog*!'

Ho ho! A warm welcome to Wales! Hmm? Marvellous!

I remember a hot one in the seventies while on holiday at 'Bide-a-wee', a little cottage we'd borrowed in Llylladdagog or somewhere – the flames quite literally licking Mrs Manager's gumboots. Marvellous!

But finally, myself and Joan had found our spiritual home! Well, our spiritual third home, I suppose, our spiritual second home having been torched even before we'd set foot in this miserable little footballing backwater.

But at last I had found success – at Cardiff! – who back then were a team mainly made up of part-timers. Owen the baker! Owen the butcher! Owen the panel-beater! Ho ho! I could go on.

Ron, are you going to go on?

No.

My proudest moment was leading the 'Cardiffers' proudly to the final of the Autoglass Windscreen Trophy. At last,

Ron Manager was bringing home the silverware! The bloomin' Autoglass Windscreen Trophy had become jammed tightly on my head during some 'hi-jinks' in the team bath. If it hadn't been for Owen the panel-beater, who knocked it back into shape, before somewhat sheep-ishly returning it to the rightful winners a few days later, we'd have been up shit cre*k! Marvellous isn't it – that's football!

Eventually, despite my successes on the pitch, I was once again shown the door, when someone secretly videoed my performance at the club karaoke night – I do quite a mean Tom Jones you know! But following my barn-storming performance of 'What's new pussycat', my rousing rendi-tion of 'Taffy was a Welshman. Taffy was a thief. Taffy came to our house and stole a lump of beef . . .' seemed to touch a raw nerve among the humourless bunch of sheep-rustlers and their dumpy wives.

Political correctness gone mad! isn't it? We learnt the bloomin' thing at school, for heaven's sake! It's not meant to be serious! Who in their right mind would come to your house and steal a lump of beef? You can't give the stuff away.

Though, to be fair, Taffy actually got a fiver for it from Owen the butcher who relabelled it and sold it on to Sainsbury's a few weeks later.

But my time in Wales was not just football, football, football. Helping out at a local eisteddfod re-awakened my ever-dormant interest in the arts. What an eye-opener! I was expecting a couple of miserable days watching a bunch of Welsh lassies hopping about in lace and stovepipe hats to a dour batch of gloomy dirges from some sour-faced miners, but no, it's an international affair! Wales welcomes the world! Well, apart from us English folk, obviously.

And it was there I was first introduced to a muscly little fellow called Michael Flatley.

'And what do you do young man?' I asked him wryly.

And he showed me. Bloomin' heck! I just laughed and laughed and laughed – Blow me! it was Irish dancing! Big Jack Charlton seemed mightily impressed – especially when he discovered Michael's chorus line didn't have one true 'colleen' among them!

'But dey all tink they're Oirish!' quipped Michael in his intriguing transatlantic drawl. Marvellous!

Well, in those days nobody had heard of the diminutive 'hoofer' who was soon to drag Irish dancing kicking and screaming on to the global stage. And 'Wor' Jackie was then best known for the scandal caused by his 'little black book' – which reputedly bore the names of every player with whom he had an unsettled score. Who would then have known what heady heights we would all attain in our chosen fields?

And as an unexpected postscript, some years later, I spent a most convivial night out in the West End with Jack and Old 'Flatters' – by now Michael was the star of *Riverdance*. Ho ho! Three red-blooded males out on the town in the heart of Theatreland! And as one of the privileged few to ever take a peek at Jack's infamous black book I can now divulge, it actually contained nothing but family trees. Within five minutes, Jack had convinced me of my Irish lineage. Bejabers! Isn't it? 'Oi'm as Oirish as the pigs in

Drogheda!' Holy Mary bloomin' Mother of God!

The night was young! After a few jars of the 'black stuff', it was off to an after-show party, and on the way, Michael's started demonstrating some of his moves, many of which were surprisingly physical – even Big Jack's a bit wary of getting stuck right in – but soon we've worked up a little routine. Marvellous! On to the party! – where I've inadvertently hoofed the Sultan of Brunei's wife up the behind, dislodging her yashmak and exposing her 'rear'. Luckily her bodyguard was there to draw a discreet veil over it, preventing an international incident. Ho ho! It's the *craic*! Marvellous – it's the way Oi tell 'em!

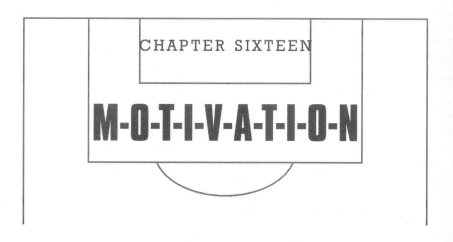

CHAPTER SIXTEEN

M-O-T-I-V-A-T-I-O-N

'. . . you *%'!*@~*%'n b*nch of wank*rs!!'

WHAT does it take to be a great football manager? Hmm? In a word, it's drive, ambition, single-mindedness and dedication! But most of all, you've got to be a motivator. At the end of the day, that's what us managers are there for, hmm? It's all very well putting your pampered professionals through their paces on the training pitch, talking team tactics till you're blue in the face, but at three o'clock on a Saturday afternoon*, that's when the real work begins.

This is what you've worked for all week, isn't it? And if you think it's now all down to the team, then you're as dim as they are.

Take it from me, if you expect to take your seat in the dugout with the *Sun* coffee-time crossword, a bottle of pop

---

★ Saturday afternoon.

and a packet of ginger-nuts, then the game's over before it's even started – not literally – but it certainly helps the first forty-five minutes pass a bit quicker.

So as soon as the ref blows his whistle, we're on our feet! Prowling the touchline like caged beasts! Bawling ourselves hoarse in impotent rage! Disputing every decision! Doing our pieces with the fourth official! Ho ho! Looks like we're barking mad, doesn't it? Well, you couldn't be more wrong. It's cool and it's calculated, and it's as much a part of the beautiful game as the sly twist of the nuts or the swallow-dive into the six-yard box favoured by the Continentals on the field of play.

But it's not all an act! We might not be out there on the pitch with the lads, but we're kicking every ball with them, making every tackle, feigning every injury, as we mercilessly harangue the pasty bunch of losers we inadvertently purchased in a panic-stricken drunken stupor from some fellow bewildered clown on the managerial merry-go-round. Marvellous!

But all the time, the trick is maintaining that 'face like thunder' to ensure that come the interval, we've put the fear of God into the useless b*ighters. Because when the half-time whistle blows, that's when the real work begins.

Who's the first person down the tunnel? You've got it in one! It's Mr Motivator – the manager! – eyes blazing, single-mindedly focused on the job in hand, brisk purposeful strides to convey that necessary air of menace – and to guarantee first place in the queue for a quick wee – Then we're headed straight for the dressing room, ready to vent our spleen – willy-nilly!

No standing on ceremony! This is our domain, and we're going to dish it out, hmm?

Whether it's one of Sir Alex's overpaid under-performing internationals quaking in his Nike Predators at the prospect of a blast from Fergie's famous hair dryer or a lowly journeyman trembling at the thought of Ron Manager's rough old bath towels, it's all the same to us. It's what we're paid for. This is where the real work begins.

Ho ho! And you wouldn't want to be a 'fly-on-the-wall', when Ron's giving the lads a 'flea-in-the-ear'.

'You're useless, you lot are! That was a rotten first half performance . . .'

Here Joan! What happened to all my effing and blinding?

Ron, we're aiming at the Christmas market you stupid c**t.

Er, fair game.

But as the last teacup whistles through the air, that's when you change tack. It's simple psychology, isn't it? This is where the real work begins.

Coaxing, cajoling – sometimes pleading – down on one knee, down on both knees, struggling manfully to our feet – sometimes slumping into the corner of the dressing room, ashen-faced, as if suffering from trapped wind. Then a few well-chosen words to send the lads back out with fire in their bellies!

'Let's get out there and show 'em what we're made of!'

'Defeat is not an option!' 'Defeat is good!' as Nelson Mandela's chiropodist used to say!

Joan, I think that's one of Big Ron Atkinson's 'funnies' – better check if we're allowed to use it.

Er, 'Cry havoc and let slip the dogs of war!' Isn't it?

Ho ho! 'Cry haddock!' I used to bawl out at Grimsby – which wasn't one of my 'funnies', it was actually a genuine mistake, but no one ever had the heart to tell me. Mind you, for all the reaction I got from the lazy, pampered, underpaid semi-professionals, I might as well have cried 'hammock' and strung a blanket up between the goal posts.

But that's the crazy world of a top football manager. Motivators, that's what we are. But having given the performance of our lives, given 101 per cent, done the business – instilling belief and confidence where once there was none – there's no better feeling than watching eleven men striding out for the second half, all geed up, fired up and raring to go.

Yet despite our hard-boiled exteriors, we're only human. Little do they know, as they shuffle out, cowed and morose, that though outwardly raging and apoplectic, the fearsome ogre of the dressing room is already shaking his head in wry amusement. We managers know it's a funny old game. Ho ho! The wholly ridiculous and pointless life of the professional sportsman! Isn't it? Marvellous!

And as the bonny lads take the field to recommence the battle, there's just a few moments left for quiet reflection, a look at the *Sun* coffee-time crossword, a bottle of pop, a packet of ginger-nuts and a quick wee before the second half. Because that's when the real work begins.

But the half-time team talk – hmm?

The football manager in full cry! Bloomin' awesome, isn't it? Giving our all! Masters of rhetoric! Motivators! Malevolently punctuating our foul and abusive bellowing with the crash of crockery – marvellous!

Of course, you need to have a couple of drinks first – not for Dutch courage – be fair, without a hint of alcohol on the breath, anyone would think we were all a bit 'cuckoo'!

And, of course, you're occasionally going to come a cropper. Arriving for a Cup tie at Yeovil a little worse for wear, I endured a strangely surreal forty-five minutes before stumbling gingerly down the famous sloping pitch into the dressing room and doing my pieces.

The players gazing sheepishly at their boots – dumb-struck! Ron Manager in his pomp! And out they went, completely unrecognisable from the team I'd sent out in the first half – at which point it dawned on me that I was in the wrong dressing room.

And as plucky Yeovil carried out my instructions to the letter, they lost their shape, lost a bit of belief – and finally the three-goal lead they'd taken in from the first half. All's well that ends well, hmm? Marvellous!

Why had nobody pointed out my error? Be fair, nobody stops Ron Manager in full flow! Ask the Somerset Constabulary – one of them completed my *Sun* coffee-time crossword as he waited to book me for indecent behaviour! Ho ho! Scrumpy, isn't it? Who'd have thought the humble Granny Smith could be turned into such a powerful weapon against the fabric of society. And this was in the days before 'crusties', 'stop the world' and dogs that pong on a bit of string.

But at the end of the day, being a manager – it's a full-time job, isn't it? That's unless you take it on part-time, obviously – otherwise it's twenty-four hours a day, seven days a week. And while the pampered playboys of the modern game slope off with their surgically enhanced supermodels, content in mid-table mediocrity, we're off to bed with pen and paper, dreaming up tactics, tossing and turning as we wonder how on earth to keep a clean sheet, quite literally.

Well we might be tossers and turners, but not always at the same time er . . . in fact, we're tusslers! Relishing the tussle! – ruminating nocturnally on our pillows . . . Er, hang on, this is all starting to sound a bit undignified.

Let Ron introduce you to the secrets of the 'inner sanctum'. Ho ho! sounds like part of the small intestine, doesn't it? Don't worry, I'm talking about the boot room – I'm not saying it doesn't smell like part of the small intestine, mind you.

But behind the scenes – that's where your number twos hold sway. Our trusty assistants, the back-room boys – the unsung heroes of the beautiful game! And though obviously not as important as us managers, they still have their tiny part to play, relieving the pressure on us hardy souls who eat, sleep, breathe and, er, wear football – twenty-five hours a day, eight days a week.

Always giving 110 per cent. Let's face it, it's a dangerous

profession, hmm? It's enough to make you pop! And that's why you can't beat a good hearty number two. We all need to loosen our load, as seventies soft rockers The Eagles so succinctly put it. Us castaways on Manager Island we need our 'Man Friday'.

Someone who'll take care of all the minor distractions such as training, tactics, strategy and team selection, yet is always there to give the players a kiss and a cuddle after the manager has done his pieces, kicked some backsides, and reduced his arrogant squad of pampered overpaid whippersnappers to a bunch of quivering jellies.

And, be fair, when I say a kiss and a cuddle, it's usually just a cuddle, although with the influx of foreigners into the modern game, maybe an affectionate little peck on the cheek or a squeeze of the metatarsal has become more prevalent. But nothing untoward – these are the trusty fellows who've probably been working with you for years. In my case, it was Big Norm! – who was actually my second number two – replacing Solomon Grundy from Sheffield Wednesday, my first 'Man Friday', who didn't even last the week, er, marvellous.

Yes, happy families, that's the stuff! It's not just effing and blinding and flinging teacups, you know! If you want to do the business where it matters – on the pitch! – you've got to put in the work behind the scenes. Football's a team game, isn't it? And team games require team spirit – that's when you turn to that strange fascination that a deck of cards holds over us footie folk.

Although I was almost seduced into this arcane world at an early age by the actor Johnny who lived next door –

Beggar Your Neighbour, wasn't it? hmm? – it was Big Norm who introduced me to the twilight world of the card school, when joining me as my assistant at Grimsby. Taking charge of a team then languishing at the foot of the table without a single clean sheet that season, our first action was to gather them all round the old card table for a good old bonding session. And although I wouldn't endorse the all-night games favoured by many England managers, if it's good for team spirit, what the heck!

However, you've got to be careful things don't get out of hand. Once, when travelling up to the Northeast with Big Norm, on the over-night train before a fifth-round Cup tie, a furious game of Happy Families ensued, which was to eventually leave me utterly drained. Norm's reluctance to concede possession of Mr Bun the Baker resulting in a fierce tussle which continued round the table in our hotel bar long into the night. At some point sheer fatigue caused me to slide off the seat in a deadly torpor. I didn't even make it to my bed! Come the morning, I was still languishing at the foot of the table. Who cares! First clean sheet of the season! Marvellous!

CHAPTER SEVENTEEN

'HOW!' IT'S THE CHEROKEE CLUB

"Twas on the good ship Venus. By hell you should have seen us, a seagull shat upon my hat. I'm off to the dry cleaners.'

FOOTBALL, hmm? If it's given me one thing in life, it's a sense of community and a sense of belonging. One big happy family, isn't it? hmm? And despite all the trials and tribulations I have had to endure, quite literally, over the years, I've always had the backing of my nearest and dearest – my family. Ho ho! My football family, not Joan, Ferenc and the other fellow, whose name escapes me right now, er, Joan introduced me to him just the other day. Well, friends may come and go, but I'll always remember the camaraderie and the great days with the Cherokee Club.

Ho ho! Not as high-brow a bunch as you're probably thinking. The Cherokee Club was not so much a celebration of indigenous culture, more a posse of red-blooded braves out on the town in the wild wild West End – blowing all our wampum on firewater and dolly-birds and, er, back to squaw one! Confused? – Let me explain a little more about this secret society of top football faces, dedicated to, you know, fun fun fun and a bit of work for charity. Much like the Freemasons, I suppose. Great stuff! And harmless, er, fun fun fun!

How did I get involved with all this, hmm? Life is in many ways like football, it's round and in just the same way as a game can turn on a few well-chosen words, so can, er, other things! For me it was a dour relegation tussle away to Jim Smith's Portsmouth. Thanks to Joan's film society having recently taken a keen interest in the Western, I had begun experimenting with my half-time motivational techniques and had taken to rallying my troops in the dressing room with a little routine based on Custer's last stand. And it seemed to do the trick. As the team listened in awe, I got quite carried away, winding up to quite a climax. 'Remember the Alamo!' I raged. Firing 'em up, before slumping back in my chair as they strode out whoopin' and hollerin' to meet their Waterloo. In retrospect maybe I had got a little overexcited, but as the stewards escorted me from the premises, I got an appreciative nod from the Bald Eagle himself.

'F**k me, it's f**kin' Little Big H*rn!'

And that was my induction to the famous Cherokee Club. Marvellous! And it wasn't just fun fun fun – we were involved in plenty of charity work as well.

Here's some personal memories from these hell-raising, fund-raising funsters from the eighties.

Navigating for Bald Eagle in the Cherokee Club's annual car rally across the Pennines, my son Ferenc tucked up on the back seat snoring contentedly, singing along with old Gentleman Jim on the four-track cartridge – Jim Reeves, I mean, not blooming Jim Smith! 'Distant Drums', isn't it? Marvellous!

'Ron, shut it and stick the radio on,' suggested Old Smithy.

'. . . and now on to the football – news is just coming in of a vacancy for the hot seat at Manchester United . . .'

Ho ho! No need to tell us Cherokee Club boys! Just at that very moment, though barely audible over the crackling of the radio and the rumble of the engine, we had heard a familiar sound and it was unmistakeable. It was the sound of distant drums! all right!

'Passing Water!' I shouted.

Jim's immediately wrestled the wheel of the big green Humber over to the hard shoulder.

It was . . . 'Passing Water' all right! . . . Martin Edwards! The Manchester United supremo! Him pounding out heap big news of vacancy at Old Trafford!

And before you can say 'How!', Jim's knocking out sparks with two dry sticks while I'm involved in a furious tussle with Ferenc over the car blanket. And cometh an hour and a half, combusteth the sticks – and we were finally sending our applications for the most coveted position in football up into the night sky! Whuff! Whuff! Whuff! Whuff! . . . WHOOOoooffff! 'Ron Manager him heap big interested in biggest job in football!'

WHOP . . . phut! 'Er, Bald Eagle – him too!'

Marvellous! Our hats were in the ring! But just as we peered expectantly into the night sky – watching the last few wisps disappearing across the Pennines – we heard the sound of squealing brakes, as another vehicle came screeching round the bend. Dammit! It's only bloomin' 'Heap Big' Ron Atkinson in his souped-up Mini Cooper! And within seconds a couple of dolly-birds have leaped out the back and are helping him out of his car coat. A few scoots of pink paraffin, a quick waft of the camel-hair overcoat and – WHUUUFFF! – he's bagged the United job! Ho ho! Great days! Big names, big characters! Big personalities! Makes the lads today look like a bunch of shrinking violets, doesn't it? hmm?

Look at the rumpus caused by Sam Hammam's harmless little stroll round the pitch. Be fair, we all used to do it in the seventies – and far more inflammatory stuff than Sam's harmless 'Ayatollah' guff. Flamboyant days, wasn't it? And we all had our trademark routines – after being struck by an artificial limb hurled from the family enclosure, I used to incite the baying hordes behind the goal to acts of mindless violence with my traditional talismanic scuttle round the pitch in the manner of Jake the Peg! marvellous!

I'll never forget a dour goalless home Cup tie against QPR – Jim Smith in his pomp! Twenty minutes left on the clock and I'm just preparing to wind up the home fans, when suddenly the Bald Eagle's bolted off anticlockwise with his familiar bang-on 'Max Wall' impersonation – with my bloomin' 'extra leg' tucked under his arm. – Bawling hysteria from Jim's travelling support, Ron's 'barmy army' shocked into stunned silence, before filing sheepishly out through the turnstiles in orderly fashion.

Great days, and a great bunch of lads! Honest Jim Smith – integrity personified! 'Honest Injun', that's the Bald Eagle. The only one who's retained his nickname from the old Cherokee Club. Um, marvellous!

'Heap Big' Ron Atkinson! Ken 'Sioux' Bates! Emlyn 'Crazy Horse' Hughes! One by one they all rode off into the sunset.

Even myself! though Ron 'Little Plums' Manager didn't so much ride into the sunset as get flung out, actually, shortly after inheriting a cowboy suit.

Despite knowing it would be frowned upon, I'd always fancied myself sitting tall in the saddle – much like John Wayne in his pomp! And though the rest of the lads initially tolerated the waistcoats and the ten-gallon hat, they drew the line at my fondness for the leather chaps.

And for all the ladies who think that there's something funny about us footie lads and our fondness for male company, to be honest, let him among us who has not the merest whiff of lavender about him raise the first eyebrow. But sometimes I have been grossly misinterpreted, so before anybody gets the wrong end of the stick, if anybody thinks that I am in any way homophobic, just ask the wife! Ron Manager has always been fiercely heterosexual. So let me take this opportunity to bolt the closet door firmly shut. It all seems to stem from a few rather ripe *double entendres* I once accidentally made at a charity dinner – no one writes their own speeches! But once the rumours start . . .

... resulting in the *News of the World*'s headline 'Who's innuendo Ron?' ... and some of the gutter press sinking so low as to quote the old terrace anthem, 'Man-a-ger, Superstar, walks like a woman ...'

For the record, I, in fact, walk like a man – much in the manner of Frankie Valli. And as for 'wearing a bra' ... ???

Well, I've got that off my chest. Let's get on with the football! It's a man's game! Ho ho – men are from Mars, women are from Venus, isn't it?

Joan, Joan! Where's that Uranus funny I had? What? It's not funny? Oh, all right.

Yes! it's a man's game! – though to be fair, I do recall the great Real Madrid team from the sixties having a number of 'confirmed bachelors' in the ranks – but that was their business. Nowadays it seems a man's private life is no longer his own. 'Outings', isn't it? hmm?

Well, even the most innocent outings can be misinterpreted by the media, and I was always brought up to respect a man's right to privacy. I've always been a stickler for it – and Big Norm ... er, he was a bit of a 'stickler' for it too!

With my reputation besmirched in the Sunday tabloids, I certainly got a bit of stick from the wife, who was understandably concerned about my gallivanting around. She didn't even want me to go down the local that day – in case I got a bit of stick from the lads as well. But let me tell you, Ron Manager wears the trousers! So after enjoying a couple of pints, me and Big Norm walked – and let me tell you Ron Manager 'uses' his walk much in the manner of Barry Gibb of the beat group The Bee Gees! Yes, me and Norm walked back from the pub to watch the top Premiership action back at Manager Towers, drooling in anticipation! Hot dog before the game? Bucket seat? Hot dog after? Ho ho! Not today! We were off to watch the game on cable TV. Joan had better have everything the way I wanted it.

An Englishman's home is his castle! isn't it? Three-seater sofa from Kingdom of Leather! Cushions all plumped up! Sunday lunch of manly roast beef and Yorkshires – swimming in gravy! Marvellous!

But blow me! – thanks to the unexpected arrival of the in-laws we've come home to find a packed house – and every bloomin' seat's already taken.

Mrs Manager's rather effete cousin offers his bloomin' knee to sit on . . .

Ho ho! 'No thanks, chum!'

But – dammit! – Norm's only bagged the bean-bag – and I've ended up on the leathery old pouffe! Hmm?

CHAPTER EIGHTEEN

THERE'S MAGIC IN THE AIR! HMM?

*'There's a one-eyed yellow idol on the er, bus to
Kathmandu . . . apparently . . .'*

LET'S face it, us football folk, we're a superstitious bunch – we always have been. Although taking the field exuding confidence and self-control, anyone witnessing the desperate arcane rituals of the dressing room in the moments leading up to kick-off will tell you a different story.

Us football folk all have our funny little ways. Take Paul Ince – the self-styled 'guv'nor' – always used to leave his shirt off till the very last minute. In similar fashion, I would never 'don' my shorts until we were about to emerge from the tunnel – once I was so 'focused' before an intense relegation tussle that I clean forgot! Ho ho! Can you picture it? Enduring image, isn't it, hmm?

There's hardly a footballer that doesn't swear by his own pre-match rituals. Even without thinking, we find ourselves attempting to recreate the precise build-up that led to our greatest triumphs, trying to recapture the magic of our finest hour – left boot on first, vest back to front, or even a last-minute pee while reciting the Lord's Prayer.

In England's finest hour, as Sir Alf's wingless wonders lined up to meet the Queen, did it even cross Her Majesty's mind that they were all still wearing the same underwear that they wore for the opening game against Uruguay? Perhaps it did . . . perhaps it didn't. Yet it was nothing uncommon! Back in the fifties at Fulham, we did exactly the same on our heroic FA Cup run, all apart from Sol Pardew, who'd celebrated our second-round pummelling of Brentford a little over vigorously.

We're all the same before a big game, aren't we? Even Ron Manager! Every Saturday morning, it was a full English breakfast, kiss the dog, a peck on the cheek for the wife, eat a sparkler and then off to the game. But that was until one memorable afternoon down at Yeovil changed everything.

Arriving fresh from Bob Nudge's stag night, I lurched on to the pitch, a little worse for wear and tear, but the minute I heard the roar of the crowd I sobered up – 'big-time', as you'd say nowadays.

And – blow me! – I've only bagged a hat-trick in the first half-hour, and following a humorous incident with a Jack Russell terrier which resulted in our goalie heading for an early bath, I've saved a penalty, and also managed to put out a small fire on the terraces. While rightfully applauded for my quick thinking and heroism, I modestly shrugged it off. The right place at the right time – isn't it? – A reluctant hero merely answering a sudden call of nature

150

My earliest out-of-body
experience – gazing from the
treetops as Aunt Dolly pushes me
round the park. Enduring image.

Yup! It's the King
of the Wild Frontier...
Davy Crockett
moonlighting for
Dyno-Rod. Marvellous.

My mother makes another of her audacious but ultimately doomed attempts to cross the road.

My brothers, Tom and Eddie... mucking about.

One of Uncle Bert's favourite party tricks was making dachshunds out of balloons – and vice versa, hmm?

Bert and I (circled) watch Bob Nudge bewilder keeper Wally Cusp with a perfectly executed bicycle kick.

HULTON ARCHIVE

Top: Young Ron.

Middle: Not Ron.

Bottom: Red Ron.

Mickey Nip – a cut above…   Sol Pardew – a snip below…

It's that man again! I always had a special relationship with the Fulham Faithful – a warm welcome from the fans on my emotional return to Craven Cottage. Marvellous.

Above: 'Boo!' Yours truly taking City keeper Ted Minge completely by surprise and bringing a touch of 'samba football' to Maine Road.

Below: 'Pick that one out the back of the net...' An unfortunate backheel by the author... own goal number two. I left Roker Park with the match ball that day!

Football ain't big enough for the both of us. Me and my old mate Jimmy Hill battle for air supremacy... in the days of the big ball! Wasn't it?

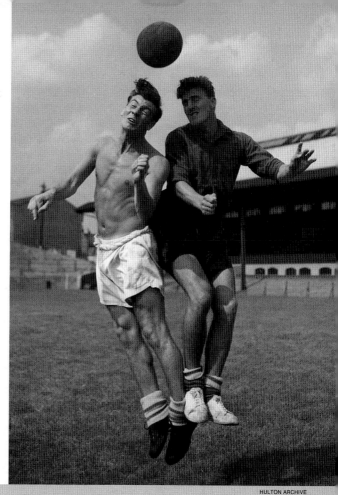

Yours truly 'hovering' in the penalty area.

A good
commentator
paints a picture...

'... oh... ooh...'

'... aw...'

'... wooargh...'

brought on by his pre-match 'hair of the dog'. Marvellous!

Ron Manager in his pomp! Weren't the seventies marvellous?

Well it's only human nature to try to recapture the unique circumstances that led to your finest hour, so from that day, on the morning of a big game, I would bawl out a few choruses of 'YMCA', before blundering into the kitchen and urinating on the fridge. Superstition, isn't it? Or just plain stupidity, hmm? Well, Mrs Manager soon knocked some common sense into me – and after a brief consultation with Gypsy Rose Lee at her caravan on Hampstead Heath, they put their heads together and came up with a more acceptable alternative for me. Subsequently, when a big match 'loomed' – is that a word? – er – you'd find me out by the rockery on the stroke of midnight, swinging a dead cat round my head three times. I managed to lose one of the blighters one night – watching despondently as it arced gracefully over the neighbour's fence – marvellous! I've still got its tail somewhere.

And if you think that it's just the players, think again! Even us top managers, though outwardly we might seem a bunch of level-headed realists, in complete control of our own destiny, for all our scheming and dreaming, we know that football's a funny old game. We might have hung up our boots but we've still got a 'footballing brain'. And no matter what contingency plans we have in place for whatever Lady Luck decides to fling at us, we've been there, done that, and seen the best laid plans of mice and manager wrecked by one wicked bobble off a divot.

From Doug Ellis's silver bullet to Big Ron Atkinson's

rabbit's foot, we've all got our lucky charms and superstitions, hmm? But when the chips are down, we clutch at straws.

If we're not carrying out exorcisms on the pitch after finding the stools in the boot room all stacked up like a game of Jenga, we're having the unlucky dressing room repainted, lighting poncey candles, enlisting the bloomin' Pope to lift a gypsy curse, or desperately hiring our own mystical charlatans – all in the hope it might make all the difference between drawing and losing.

Look at Uri Geller – feverishly manipulating the results down at Reading. Mrs Manager frequently has trouble with the cutlery drawer after Uri's hard-hitting programme on Radio Four – and it takes some sorting out! If only Uri could harness his undoubted talents and do something slightly more constructive – what a wonderful world it would be, hmm?

I had dinner with Uri recently and he was marvellous company, kept me enthralled all night, but just as he was about to divulge a few of his secrets over dessert – ho ho! – my spoon buckled alarmingly, and my rice pudding went for a Burton!

Joan? That was one of my 'funnies', where's all the 'bender' stuff gone? Joan? Are you there?

But belief is an important part of success on the pitch. When Jack Charlton was in charge of Ireland, half the team believed in fairies and little men, and were completely convinced they were Irish!

'Believe the magic in your mind!' isn't it? Marvellous! And if you think I'm talking 'guff' – ask yourself why Glenn Hoddle 'eschewed' the old Ouija board in favour of 'everyday housewife' Eileen Drewery – that bewildering blend of faith healing, mysticism and down-to-earth bloody-mindedness brought all sorts of 'belief' to the England camp. Mind you, they had a head-start, David Beckham still believes in Father Christmas!

And look how Glenn transformed Spurs on making his triumphant return to his spiritual home – White Hart Lane, ho ho! His methods might be a little unconventional but he's managed to restore Tottenham to their rightful position of mid-table mediocrity, hmm?

It's all down to confidence. 'You've got to bring out the magic in your mind!' When I heard the usually self-assured Teddy Sheringham bleating, 'We can't switch it on and off at will', it brought back memories of my ill-considered introduction of 'positive thinking' to Fulham in the sixties – all of us sitting glumly in a darkened dressing room staring at the light bulb, brows furrowed with grim positivity, resulting in no more than a powerful headache for myself, and the St John Ambulance carrying off two of our defenders with brain-fever. Marvellous!

And for all the ignorant sniggering about Glenn's allegedly 'wacky beliefs', you didn't hear a murmur from the press when Sven-Goran Eriksson turned up in England with his very own snake-oil merchant, Dr Willi Railo. The Swedish Svengali and Dr Willi have been in harness for twenty years – and no one dismisses Sven as a mystical 'tosser'.

And just like Glenn and Eileen, Sven and Dr Willi know how to get results. I've got to be a bit careful on intellectual rights here – you can't just hoik big lumps out of other people's books, hmm?

So let's just take a quick glimpse at his methods.

If Sven's been landed with a striker who's lost all confidence, he just hauls him by the lug round to Dr Willi, who hands the soppy fellow a pen and a piece of paper, and tells him –

'Draw me what you see when you take a penalty.'

A little humming and hawing, and he sketches a small goal and a massive goalie. Hah! Simple – it's all in the mind!

Dr Willi works his tricks on the fellow's brain, and when asked to repeat his drawing three months later, the striker merely draws a yawning net. And the next time he saunters up to the penalty spot? BANG! It's in the bottom corner.

It's the magic in your mind, isn't it? Confidence tricks! Reminiscent of Eileen Drewery in her pomp – ask Glenn! Don't think we need to be careful on intellectual rights here! – ho ho! Remember Psycho, hmm? Not Glenn – Stuart Pearce! Those mighty thighs! Reminiscent of Nijinsky in his pomp! – the racehorse, I mean, not the over-endowed maestro of the levitating ballet tights. Who can forget Stuart's abject penalty miss in Italia '90? Confidence at rock bottom. But after a few sessions round Eileen's crystal ball, he swaggers back up to the spot, and with a mighty thump hits it perfectly – BANG! – it takes a wicked deflection off a big rabbit called Harvey and – BOOF! – it's in row Z!

Joan, is it me or has it got a bit chilly in here? Joan?

Brrrrr! Where was I? Oh yes, all that magic in your mind guff – we're a right soppy bunch, hmm? from the unlucky dressing room at the Millennium Stadium to the curse of Manager of the Month.

And yes, I have supped from the poisoned magnum. I did bag the bubbly one month and before Joan had dug her box of 'accursed' Waterford crystal champagne flutes out of the cupboard under the stairs, I found myself battling a plague of locusts in Mrs Manager's greenhouse!

But Manager of the Month? Hmm? Does it bring bad luck, or is it just more superstitious twaddle*? Be fair, a bit of grudging recognition from the FA – it's hardly the curse of the pharaohs, is it? You fall foul of the pharoahs, and you're f*****! But talking from experience, if given a choice between an unwelcome slap on the back from Soho Square and the malevolent attention of the embalmed, stuffed ancients, it's 'six of the other', and er, half a dozen!

I'll never forget one of my mid-eastern junkets in the company of a rather well-known football face. It was all a bit hush-hush – we travelled under pseudonyms – him as Gerry Venables, myself as Len Bates. Well, it's a long story, but I'll keep it brief. One of Gerry's old 'friends' had invited him to take control of Valley of the Kings FC, whose previous manager had robbed them blind and left them languishing at the foot of the division. But on arrival he's decided it's not enough of a challenge – and though intrigued by their chairman's scheme to dupe tourists into buying time shares on the Great Pyramid at Thebes, he's given them the bum's rush! Pyramid selling? Not El Gel! Takes a bit of a leap of the imagination, doesn't it? Ho

---

* Balderdash.

ho! Football's the same the world over – marvellous!

But although just another week in the life for one of football's most celebrated characters, for myself it became a descent into the furthest pit of hell. For days I was confined to my bed, beset by monstrous hallucinations, sweating profusely and babbling feverishly at a red-haired little devil who I imagined to be squatting on the far end of the bed – arms folded, tormenting me constantly – suddenly shooting into the air – only to suddenly re-appear on my headboard, taunting me with, 'We wiz rrrrubbish! We wiz rrrrubbish!'

Only years later did I realise that in my delirium I'd somehow conjured up a vision of wee Gordon Strachan in his pomp! Ho ho! Only joking!

No you wisnae.

Eh? Who's that?

You ken who I am, Ron.

Help! Joooaan! I'm coming to bed.

We wiz rrrrubbish, Ron!

No you – er – we wasn't! Er . . . But if you're talking about magic, you can't get more magic than the FA Cup! Er, how's that for a link, eh, Joan?

Blindin', Ron! But it's no' Joan.

Help!

CHAPTER NINETEEN

HANDS ON THE SILVERWARE

'Ooohhh! . . . The ball comes to Ron Manager on the right! . . . Manager beats one man . . . he beats two . . . moves inside . . . Ohhh! He's punted it over the bar!'

HO HO! The romance of the Cup, hmm? Marvellous! Small boys' dreams of Wembley glory! Isn't it? hmm? But sadly the 'Manager Final' was never to be. And so it remained the one honour that would elude me in my glittering career. Never would I experience the warmth and banality of the civic reception. That first experience of the neighbourhood around the stadium, waving to cheering drunken clowns from the upper deck of the open-top bus, through unfamiliar streets, thronged with exultant hordes who've never heard of you, all flushed with civic pride, as they cheer the homecoming heroes. The FA Cup, isn't it? Possibly the most overrated bloomin' trophy in the world of football. They can stick it up their jumper as far as I'm concerned.

Bah! And if Uncle Bert's reading a copy of this up in that great stadium in the sky, I'm sorry I never won that medal for Great-Uncle Bill . . . but the most savoured trophy in football? . . . Bah! Say what you like, it's the most unhygienic bloomin' thing you could ever put in your trophy cabinet – think about it!

The number of uncouth wasters who've supped bubbly out of it, the greasy-haired morons who've worn the lid on their heads, the overpaid dolts who've flung it around the dressing room before dunking it in the polluted waters of the team bath.

If Little Wisey hasn't peed in it, I'll eat my hat! – hard-hitting stuff, hmm? Only joking Dennis!

But no regrets! Even if I had returned home with the Cup, I doubt Joan would have allowed it in the house. It would have languished out in the shed with the lucky underpants I wore for the duration of that plucky Cup run in '58, possibly on the shelf next to 'Bloaty' – Mrs Manager's Chihuahua – one of my early attempts at taxidermy, in the days before I could afford a decent set of scales to calculate the required poundage of sawdust.

But let's not get too carried away here. The FA Cup? hmm? It's nothing less than football's 'Crown Jewels' – imagine the sense of pride as you put it on your head! I always fancied the lid myself. And although it may have lost a bit of its gloss nowadays, what with the influx of foreign players and managers, unaware of its place in history, you try telling that to the fans!

Down the years, what other sporting event has provided as many treasured memories as the FA Cup final, hmm?

Magic summer days of bunting and bubbly! – the pink horse! – delirium tremens! – the pink elephant! – Help! – Charlie! – don't leave me here! – Er . . .

Ron, get a grip.

Er, and the day this magnificent competition left the old Empire Stadium, and headed off down Wembley Way, bound for gridlock and the retractable roof at the mobile home of football, who among us did not shed a tear as we bid fond farewell to the famous Twin Towers?

Ron Manager, for one! Good riddance! isn't it? They'd always made me feel a bit uneasy. Big dark horrible things, casting those long black shadows – that slight smell of damp, hmm? Well, OK, wee.

But when it came to the auctioning off of the family silver, I was there with the rest of football's great and good, all of us hoping to secure a timeless souvenir of England's heritage. We'd endured the fixtures, now we were after the fittings! Ho ho! Beat that! Marvellous!

Down to the Wembley auction night, hoping to bag a row of the famous seats, perhaps to provide a partially obscured view of Mrs Manager's rockery from the back patio – the bidding was going to be fierce!

And who was I sitting next to? – only Bobby Charlton! and I was privileged to 'eavesdrop' as he patiently demonstrated to an enthralled David Beckham how his famous hairstyle still offered the modern footballer the best of both worlds. Quite the football evangelist, isn't he, hmm? A private conversation, but I'll give you the 'gist' (don't worry

159

Bob! – I've edited the 'salty' language!).

'Although when heading a ball coming at you heavy with mud, the bare bone of the slap-headed footballer is your only man, it can be a distinct disadvantage when trying to secure an advertising contract for shampoo. When sporting the 'side-mohican', the barnet transforms into a full head of hair, with just one quick flick of the wrist!' Ho ho! Great stuff!

Apparently Sir Bob took out a patent on it back in the sixties – not thick is he? eh?

Unfortunately Bobby's demonstration innocently upped the bidding on lot ten, costing the money-men of Barcelona a few extra pesetas for the steps to the royal box. I bet that went down a bundle at the Nou Camp! As for my hilarious re-enactment of the misunderstanding which inadvertently secured me the famous Wembley urinals? . . . hmm – 'Yours truly' certainly wasn't 'flavour of the month' when Pickfords turned up at Manager Towers, er, marvellous.

Still the day wasn't a complete washout. Later that evening, I bumped into Terry Venables and spent a pleasant time exchanging wistful reminiscences of our days treading the hallowed turf at the old Empire Stadium. Be fair, monstrous carbuncle or not, the playing surface was second to none – and the square patch of historic Wembley turf which now takes pride of place in Mrs Manager's rockery is in exactly the same condition as the day I bought it off Terry outside B&Q. Joan reckons it looks like it's come straight out of a butcher's shop window!

Footie fans throughout the world understand the appeal

of the greatest knockout tournament in the world. What other sporting event can attract an audience of millions throughout the world – aside from beach volleyball, hmm? The FA Cup! It's still the greatest knockout tournament in the world, isn't it? And at the end of the day, it's all about getting your hands on the silverware. Ho ho! And when I say 'silverware', I'm not talking about Ron's patented double-stitched disco pants! (Still available by mail order in size XXXL from www.ronsstrides@shorpe.com. Sorry, I'll give you the address again – from www.ronsstrides@shorpe.com – er, hang on –

Joan, what's happening here?

But once Johnny Foreigner gets his first sniff of the atmosphere of a Cup final, he's got the bug. Just ask Nwo Kanu, dreaming of banging one in for the nal? Er, sorry, that's Nwo Kanu banging one in for the nal. Eh? Dammit! Even ne Wenger remained apatheti il he realised . . . Bloomin' heck!

Ron, you've bunged on the obscenity checker.

Eh? Ho ho! Well, fuck my old boots!

Let me just give you that address again, www.ronsstrides@ scunthorpe.com.

Right ho! We're off again! What is the romance of the Cup? Hmm? What magic ingredient sets it apart from the rest? In a word, it's giant-killing. David and Goliath! Plucky David, armed only with a sling, probably clad in nothing more than a loin-cloth – a potential banana-skin for mighty Goliath, isn't it? Powerful image, hmm? A little troubling perhaps – but young boys, isn't it? Loin-cloths for goal-posts . . . ho ho marvellous! . . . ho ho . . . er . . .

The minnows taking on the big fish in a ploughed field with a sharp incline! The pampered professional chasing a hopeful punt upfield, only to see the ball stop dead in a puddle, as he carries on sliding foolishly by. Marvellous!

Have modern playing surfaces taken away some of the excitement of the beautiful game, hmm? Players slithering around hopelessly in the mud, reminiscent of Torville and Dean in their pomp. Cherished memories! – until ultimately Joan confiscated the video. Er, where was I?

Yes, the romance of the Cup! isn't it? A one-off, sudden-death, blood and thunder knockout competition, and to your ordinary, genuine, half-witted football fan, every team's in with a chance – marvellous!

We dream the impossible dream! Think the unthinkable thought! Ponder the imponderable – er, ponderings! Eat the inedible hot dog! Chase the wild elusive butterfly of love!

We relish the thought of the minnows of the Nationwide giving the big fish of the Premiership a right good kicking. We all love an underdog! ho ho, don't worry, it's only a figure of speech – I've always found it difficult to appreciate the charm of the south end of a north-bound boxer dog – slightly unsavoury image, isn't it, hmm? And I do apologise if I have unwittingly caused you to picture it in your mind's eye – er, in all its livid pomp.

But in the end, success on the pitch is measured by the contents of the trophy cabinet hmm? – From the season's

traditional curtain raiser, the Intertoto Cup, to the big one!
– the Charity Shield! Let's have a look at some of the most
coveted prizes in the world of football, hmm? – here we go!

Though often regarded as a pointless kickabout in
blinding sunshine, if you're looking for something to stick
in front of the team photo, you can't beat the Charity
Shield to cover up the close-season paunch. It's like a big
plate, isn't it? Didn't Virginia Wade win it once at the
height of punk rock? Those were the days, weren't they?
Women in short skirts wearing proper pants! ho ho! – not
those little bits of string they favour nowadays. Remember
Yvonne Goolagong? The queen of the billabong! Under
the shade of the coolibah tree wasn't it? Er, sorry . . . Yes,
the Charity Shield! er, it's always the same woman who
presents it, isn't it? What's her name . . . ?

Joan, you must know this one.

Sorry, Ron, I'm miles away, I can't stop thinking about that dog's
arse.

Er, neither can I.

Come on, who is it? Er, the Duchess of something – you
know, the pretty one with blonde hair! Lady Penelope?
'Yuss m'lady!' Marvellous!
    Er . . . let's move on to the Intertoto Cup. Ho ho! It
sounds like a little dog, doesn't it?
    'Oo-err, I don't think we're in Kansas anymore . . .
Auntie Em! Auntie Em!'

Ron, I told you – get a grip.

Er right, that'll do. What else? The UEFA Cup! hmm? The hokey-cokey of the club competitions! – Champions League – you're in – 1st leg out! – the UEFA Cup you're in – second leg out! – marvellous. Great stuff!

They're all a bit Mickey Mouse these trophies, aren't they? Your Europeans just don't have our sense of history and tradition.

How about the Worthington Cup? – So good they named it lots of times!

The Milk Cup! Littlewoods Cup! Rumbelows Cup! Er, Coca-Cola Cup? Wasn't it? Hmm? But Mickey Mouse? Don't make me laugh! He always did make me laugh actually – always up to something, wasn't he? Remember those big feet, and no matter what way he turned, those big ears that always seemed to be facing you, hmm? Er, Gary Lineker in his pomp, wasn't it? Who cares? Getting your hands on the silverware? Be fair, at the end of the day, if you don't make it into the Champions League, none of it's worth a flying ***k, hmm? Marvellous!

Is that it, Ron?

I can't think of any more.

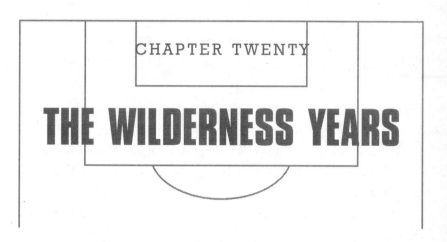

CHAPTER TWENTY

THE WILDERNESS YEARS

'I'd rather have a flottal obottamy, than a fottal ablottamy! Isn't it?'

'Ron, we heard you the third time.'

RON Manager – hell-raiser, wit and raconteur! My appearances on the *Parkinson Show* had turned me into a national institution, attracting record viewing figures as I held audiences spellbound with my hilarious anecdotes and verbal dexterity. Yet even as millions of viewers tuned in to be regaled by Ron Manager – in his pomp! – behind the façade, this fun-loving, hard-drinking *bon viveur* was actually 'off his chump'.

Though funnily enough, despite my increasingly erratic behaviour, I don't think Joan ever noticed, bless her heart. Without meaning to be offensive in any way, women are thick, hmm?

My life had become a giddy round of chat shows, charity

fund-raising dinners and opening nights. A life played out in front of an adoring public – and it was mighty heady stuff for a lad from Burnt End. This was a whole new world – Ron was 'beloved'.

The adulation was intoxicating, and I was drawn to it like a moth to a flame. Yet even as I flew closer to the sun, the wax holding my, er, tail feathers* had begun to melt, and without me being aware of it, my behaviour had begun to spiral out of control. Welcome to the wilderness years, wasn't it? Hmm?

Looking back, I had lost it! What had I lost? I had no idea. Even had I found it, I'd have been none the wiser, and I'm not.

My life had become a blur – and in my stupor I no longer had a grip on what was reality and what pure fantasy. Did it really happen or did I dream it? Ridiculous situations still come back to me as large as life – preposterous notions surely conjured from the depths of my alcoholic delirium.

'Oonhand it, yoong man!'

'I won't! I won't!'

Did I really wake up in a ditch by the side of the road, tussling furiously over a can of Mackeson with Cloughie?

Did I really take Ferenc's rounders bat from the boot of the car and clump a future England manager round the head as he enjoyed forty winks in a lay-by? – and all just for fun? Or were they all the absurd and fantastical imaginings of a fevered brain, brought to the edge of insanity by the demon drink? **c* knows.

---

* To my arse feathers.

But even as my popularity soared, reality had begun to descend. I was walking the giddy tightrope of excess without a safety net, and I was destined for a fall. Making my way back from TV Centre one night, I arrived at Paddington just as the last train wheezed out of the station, and wearily folding my clothes neatly by the side of a bench, I settled down for a quick night-cap and a kip under my newspaper. 'G'night Ron' I said. 'G'night' I replied.

What's black and white and red and blew all over? er, it's not one of my 'funnies' – it was my newspaper. Woken up shivering by a guardian of the law – buck naked – er, me, I mean, not the guardian of the law! Nursing a shocking hangover and with only the faintest recollection of my hilarious appearance on Parkie – the guardian of the law that is, not me! – I could clearly recall flirting outrageously with some Australian woman called Barry or Humphrey or something, and then was it on to the Pillars of Hercules? – possibly 'besting' Oliver Reed at arm wrestling . . . ?

It was all starting to come back to me . . . spurred on by my success, I had taken up his face-saving challenge, and found myself pitted against the burly hell-raising thespian in a ferocious one-to-one contest of physical might and dexterity, merely in order to determine once and for all which one of us was most 'hard'.

Who came out on top? Who do you think? Despite Ollie's desperate gamesmanship – it takes more than a bit of snoring to distract Ron Manager from the job in hand! – ask the wife!

But now, coming to my senses with one arm still stiff from the wrestling, the other buried deep in a tub of Chicken McNuggets, I knew I did not feel 110 per cent. To put it bluntly, Ron Manager was not quite in his pomp. The morning after the Lord Mayor's Show, isn't it? hmm? This time it looked like I was done up like a kipper! And with my 'one-armed press-ups' explanation incorrectly interpreted by the policeman as a euphemism for 'God-alone-knows-what', I knew I was 'done up big-time'.

'Look, you've had a long night. Why don't you just get yourself home and have some kip?'

Ho ho! It's only bloomin' worked! Marvellous, hmm? You can't trust your specials like your old-time coppers, isn't it? He's sloped off and left me to my own devices – some of which I didn't even remember taking out with me! A couple of them actually belonged to Joan! ho ho!

Shut it, Ron.

OK.

So, a quick nip from the hip flask, a mild altercation in Burger King, and home to an empty house to find a terse note from Joan, 'Ron, I've had enough, you can stick it up your ars*, I'm off to shag Ken Bates.'

What? That snake in the grass! – I was devastated! Who wouldn't be? Yet after a few hours of recuperation, I realised I had completely misread the note. Joan was off to shag Len Bates! It wasn't the Chelsea chairman, it was the fellow from Bates' Bathrooms, who'd recently retiled our 'smallest room' – the bloomin' local plumber! Suddenly, big-shot or not, I knew I was no longer Charlie Big Potatoes. I wasn't even Charlie Potatoes.

I was a Charlie – a proper Charlie . . .

All right, Ron, leave it out.

Yet again I found myself cast adrift and alone in the world. But what is it about the professional footballer that makes him utterly irresistible to the fairer sex, hmm? Since time immimmmimmeno – since time imbemmorium – er, since emoriable –

Ever since time began, a fellow in skimpy shorts, punting a pig's bladder around for money, has attracted the attentions of the ladies. I used to have to beat them off with a p****** stick! And though perhaps not in the same league as your Ginolas or your Beckhams, I was quite a catch in my day – possibly second only to Georgie Best!

Old Bestie, hmm? Whatever it was, he had it! And so did I – I still do, if I could only lay my hands on it!

I saw quite a lot of Georgie in the twilight of his career. And having in many ways always been in the twilight of my career, I think he looked on me as a father figure. But Georgie set pulses racing, didn't he? hmm? And he still has that twinkle in his eye – isn't it? marvellous! It takes me back to those wild, wild, wild, wild nights – and wild, wild nights they, er, were were, wasn't it? Wasn't it? Marvellous! Marve – aw bloomin' heck!

---

* Pointy.

And without wanting to be controversial – and on my honour, this is not me trying to secure a big fee for the serialisation rights in some grubby tabloid! – but be fair, the Welsh Wizard could put it away! – I could put it away as well! . . . er, as long as I was asked politely!

Where was I? Yes! Georgie! 'El Beatle'!

One night I met him, purely by chance, in the bar at the Catford Hilton, just down the road from the Rivoli Ballroom – my old 'stumping ground', literally!

(Ho ho! Don't worry, it's just one of my 'funnies'.)

Two kindred spirits! Playboys of the Western world! Wine, women and song, isn't it? Marvellous!

'What are you doing here?'

'Ho ho! What are you doing here?'

Riveting stuff, hmm? Marvellous! And that's verbatim!

Joan, check 'verbatim', I have absolutely no idea what it means.

Ron, I don't get your last 'funny' – that 'stumping ground' stuff.

Good call! Er, neither do I – if it's not one of my 'funnies', just take it out.

But Georgie, isn't it? hmm? What a coincidence! Who'd have thought that two colossuses* of the football world would bang into each other, out of the blue, in a seedy hotel in Catford, and discover we'd booked adjoining suites? A pair of swingers on a summer's evening in the

---

* Big people.

heart of town, marvellous, it wasn't going to be long before we were spotted by some of the local talent. And sure as your life, just on last orders, a couple of dolly-birds come sidling up – 'show-girls', isn't it? you can tell them a mile off! We're in like – well, like Flynn it always was in my day – I don't know if that means anything to you young 'uns, but whatever you call it, we were bloomin' in there, wherever it was!

'El Beatle' laying on the charm, while 'El Barron Knight' idly chatted up a tall leggy blonde – marvellous! – French name – I'll remember it in a minute – I'd noticed her the minute she strode into the bar, confident and poised, with a figure like a super-model – and I don't mean one of those scrawny bints you get nowadays – big and buxom! – broad-shouldered, with hands like shovels – all woman! She looked like she'd walked straight off the cover of *Women's Realm* – er . . . 'Ding-dong!'

I glanced over at George. The bar was closing, but the night was young. It was time to place our order for room service. A crafty wink to the barman, and the sly tap of the nose which means 'the usual'.

He knows the score! Sly wink, reciprocal tap of the nose – and our trollies are stacked. Marvellous!

No names, no pack drill, eh? One–nil!

And me and George have sloped off to our rooms with the crumpet. Ho ho! At last, Ron's pulled! Marvellous!

Frantic tussling on the chaise longue – furious wrestling on the deep-pile rug – strange rumbling – faint banging –

'Ron! Is that your trollies?'

'Eh?' Ho ho! It's room service! Phew!

'Two magnums of bubbly for Mr Best?'

'He's next-door, you pillock!' I quipped wittily.

Alone again! Humble apologies – frantic tussling – more apologies – more faint banging – er, more apologies. Ah! It's bloomin' room service again! At last!

'Er, just stick it on the ottoman, laddie – here's a couple of bob . . .'

Then suddenly that look of recognition.

'Fuc* me, it's Ron Manager! Where did it all go wrong, Ron?'

Cheeky pup! Ho ho! Well, you just had to laugh! 'Where did it all go wrong?'!!? And me sitting there in my paisley dressing gown, with two bottles of Toby bitter, a brace of saveloys and a strapping blonde! Blow me! It doesn't get any better, does it? Hmm?

What a night! 'Once, twice, three times a lady!' as seventies heart-throb Lionel Richie used to croon! Three and a bit, if my memory serves me right – unforgettable! And I've still got her photo somewhere, signed with lipstick! 'To Ron with Luv, Danii La Rue'.*

★ (I must point out that if any of Mrs Manager's close friends are reading this, we were in fact separated at the time and, as I have explained to Joan, the publishers have stressed that without a chapter containing a few racy revelations of this nature, it is most unlikely that any grubby tabloid is likely to fork out a fat fee for the serialisation rights. And she's well aware that if I hadn't bunged this in, it would have had to have been Joan's infatuation with Tom Jones which led to her mistaken night of passion with Eddie Large – and bang goes our caravan holiday on the Isle of Wight.)

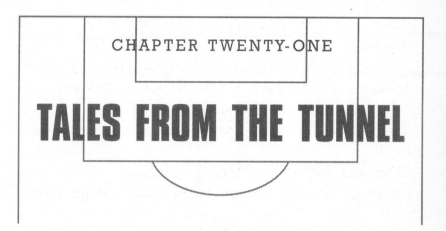

CHAPTER TWENTY-ONE

TALES FROM THE TUNNEL

*'Ho ho! My wife doesn't understand me, isn't it, hmm?
Your hair's very silky –'*

EH? Hang on a minute –

Joan, not that one again – where's that one about me bowling down the road to Damascus? You know, where I've just got myself a bubble-perm and two fellows with baseball bats knock me off my donkey when I'm snoozing in a lay-by, and all that 'mistaken identity' guff? Joan?

It's a funny old game, isn't it? Hmm? We walk through this crazy world alone, don't we? blinkered and blind-folded, isn't it? taking everything in our stride, living our lives in the public eye, trudging despondently from every ignominious defeat to each new public humiliation, trying to make sense of our wholly pointless existence –

– bloomin' miserable – our only reason for living, our terror of the beyond . . .

Ron, buck up, or go to bed.

Joan! You're back!

Ron, I was on the toilet.

Yes! But even in our darkest hour, even as we've resigned ourselves to walk cowed and beaten into that black night, suddenly – boooff!

That sudden something occurs which changes your life forever. And so it came to, er, pass for Ronald Ivanhoe Manager.

A grudge match at Anfield! wasn't it? hmm? Liverpool taking on their deadliest rivals – Manchester United! Marvellous!

The Mighty Reds go head-to-head against, the, er, Mighty Reds! For once an innocent bystander, I sat cross-legged on the fence, rubbishing both teams with equanimity, as I awaited the blessed relief afforded by the advert break.

Returning from my half-time wee, I paused momentarily by the visitors' dressing room. The door slightly ajar, I lingered a while and listened as Sir Alex gently cajoled his team into improving on their first-half performance.

'*Pock!*'

Ho ho! There goes a teacup! Here we go! Wait for that first blast from the famous hair dryer . . .

'Ye useless tubes, you couldnae hit a coo's erse wie a banjo!'

Great stuff. Business as usual, isn't it?

'*Claash!!*'

That'll be a saucer!

'*Paaarp!*' – er, someone breaking wind, possibly Keano or Fergie himself, seeing as nobody laughed.

'*Claash!!*' Ho ho! There goes another saucer! Eh? What happened to the teacup? Not like Sir Alex to vary his routine, hmm? Intrigued, I poked my head round the door –

'*Pock!!*'

I suddenly received a terrific blow to the head, which put me right on my behind! I staggered to my feet, dazed and confused – where was I? – I had complete control of my senses – I could still hear the reassuring sound of those familiar, Caledonian ravings, yet now they seemed oddly muffled and strangely distant. One deep breath told me I was still in the players' tunnel, and though reeling from the honk of liniment and oxter*, I slowly pulled myself together.

My vision was unimpaired, yet I felt as if in some way I was looking down on myself. For the first time in my whole life, I was aware of a small bald patch on the crown of my head, and how my right ear sat a couple of inches further forward than my left – intriguing stuff, isn't it? hmm?

But even as I hastily gathered my bearings, I found myself drawn by a blinding light towards the end of the tunnel, emerging to a strange yet familiar landscape – football

---

* Scottish and Northern English – a person's armpit.

pitches stretching as far as the eye could see – a bit like Hackney marshes in fact, yet without the familiar sound of laboured breathing and inane obscenity as fat old lads kick lumps out of each other under sullen skies. Suddenly it dawned on me – the awful realisation that I had passed over to the other side – Ron was only in bloomin' heaven! What a result! One–all, isn't it, hmm?

Had I deserved this? Although I had always tried to tread the rightful path, I had always expected to spend a little time in Purgo – er – in Limbatory – you know, wher-ever you're supposed to end up when you get caught out and, you know, when your sins come on top.

As so often before, I stood dumbfounded and distracted. Luckily St Peter's lunged in and pitched me straight into a celestial game of 'three and in' – Pearly Gates for goal-posts, isn't it? And Ron's in top company! Marvellous!

Moore to Manager! 'On me head, lad!' – Manager to Matthews – to St Peter! – 'dooooh!' – 'You Wanker!' – 'O Gabriel come blow your horn!'

Then – blow me! – I'd seen that dizzying turn before, it's my old mucker from my Fulham days – Chris Pipe!

The centrifugal centre-half! His left peg was just for standing on! No, really it was – it was bloomin' wooden!

But Chris Pipe? He could run rings round anyone – as long as it was in an anticlockwise direction, owing to his artificial limb being slightly shorter than his good leg, mar-vellous! Then, one summer on a pre-season tour 'down under', after an intense exhibition match against Ayers Rock FC, I remember watching him strangely intrigued by the water draining from the plughole in the team bath. Ho ho.

The southern hemisphere, isn't it, hmm? Bloomin' peculiar!

The very next game, Chris set off in a clockwise manner and we never saw him again. 'He's probably been eaten by dingoes!' I quipped – and it turns out he bloomin' had! Well blow me! I was made up. There was one in the eye for all those 's*art al*cs'. Ho ho! Who's a 't*****t' now?

But even as I savoured the moment of my most glorious triumph, I felt suddenly dizzy. My head was swimming – literally! Er . . .

Ron, do you want me to take that 'literally' out?

Joan, no, hang on.

My head was spinning – literally! Whirling earthward, my off-set ears acting much as the rotors of a paper helicopter. Yet even as I plummeted, I could hear a faint voice calling my name . . .

'Ron . . . Ron . . .'

I woke as if from a dream.

'Och dammit! Ah thocht* ye wis deid**! It wis jist wan o' ma teacups son***! Sumtimes ma aim's as bad as they chanty-wrastlers**** on the pitch!'

Ron was back! And from then on I had no fear of the after-life, knowing that one day I would take the field with

---

* Thought.

** You was dead.

*** I'll accept the blame for the crockery.

**** The useless tubes couldnae hit a coo's erse wie a banjo.

those legendary names – Mickey Nip, Sol Pardew, Mark Pitts, Eddie Cleak, Chris Pipe, Bob Nudge, Cliff Richards, Terry Pop . . . and, er, Boothby Swipe if he hasn't gone to the 'other place' – marvellous.

And without coming over all sanctimonious, I now returned to the beautiful game with a new perspective and a sense of history and insight, determined that I was going to put my life in order. I had been returned for a reason, my work on earth was unfinished!

I had a career and a marriage to save, and I strode out with a new sense of purpose. If I put my skates on, I could get a pint in before *Match of the Day*.

As the years fly by, I often picture myself looking down benevolently from the celestial dugout, watching football fans throughout the country standing glumly in reverent silence as they struggle to come to terms with my demise.

The stressful life of the football manager, isn't it, hmm? Be fair, it's the biggest job in the world, and we can't last forever! I've said it before and I'll say it again –

We eat, sleep, breathe and, er, wear football! Twenty-five hours a day! Eight days a week!

Even Ron manager can't last forever. But no regrets – we make our beds, and we bloomin' lie in 'em!

So when God finally brandishes the red card, let's have no long faces – no minute's silence. Let's have a 'minute's racket' for Ron!

Lusty cheering! 'Oggi oggi oggi!' Maybe a quick chorus of 'For he's a jolly good fellow!' Then wheeeep! – enough! – 'Ron is dead, long live the Ron!'

On with the football! Marvellous!

CHAPTER TWENTY-TWO

LEARNING TO FLY!

*'Look . . . look, Ron! He's put his foot in the cat tray!
. . . Ooh! . . . Hee hee! . . . He's pulled the radiator off
the wall! . . . Look Ron, he's set his trousers on fire!
. . . Hee hee hee!'*

BLOOMIN' heck! Mrs Manager's watching *Mr Bean* –
marvellous, hmm – isn't it? – peein' herself! A far cry from
the welcome I received on my return from my legendary
'lost weekend' – and Joan's reaction on finding the seat of
my best slacks scorched from my ill-advised demonstration of the combustible properties of methane!

But it knocked some sense into me, and from that day
on*, even if I hadn't changed my ways overnight** I
became more aware of my responsibilities to my family,

★ Tuesday
★★ Tuesday night/Wednesday morning.

and I became a secret drinker! To my shame, Joan was none the wiser, and, oblivious to the glazed expressions of myself and her friends, spoke proudly of my new regime of exercise and abstinence. To be fair she did point out that the beneficial effects were even more marked in the sleeker contours of Eddy, our dachshund.

So every night, I raucously swigged 'dandelion and burdock' from the bottle, and harangued the television, before tottering out into the street, to hurl abuse at the neighbours and 'walk the dog'. Marvellous!

In the end, I was hurting no one but myself – though I felt the occasional pang of guilt when I saw the lean and hungry look in Eddy's eyes, as the weight continued to fall off him, having secretly halved his supply of Kennomeat in order to cement the deception of our energetic three-hour walks (er, sorry Eddy, wherever you are).

But one night, as I hauled a reluctant Eddy through the doors of the Old Pig, I saw a familiar face sitting in the snug . . Not 'Bustling' Bob Nudge? It couldn't be! I hardly recognised him! 'Bumbling Bob Paunch' I used to call him! Once the archetypical, burly, beer-and-fags midfielder, now here was my old pal, trim, coherent and muscular – engrossed in his book, with nothing more than an orange juice and a big Cohiba. Bob had been to hell and back.

'What did you come back for . . . forget your fags?' I quipped. But no! He's taken the pledge and he's off the pop! He'd been there, done that – wrapped it in his newspaper and put it behind him – 'Bustling' Bob Nudge! – marvellous!

We talked of old times – we had a lot to catch up on!

Ho ho! The night was young! – and he bored me shitless*
till closing time.

But as he watched me forcibly ejected into the street,
he's only lobbed his book at me with a cheery 'Take that
Ron' – it was Tony bloomin' Adams's autobiography –
and Bob bade me goodnight, adding cryptically, 'Ron,
every day's my Cup final these days!'

Well, hands up who among us hasn't lingered a little
while in Satan's fiery parlour. Hmm? Bob was hardly the
first footballer to struggle with his demons – personally,
I'd tussle with anyone's! And funnily enough, I spent a
particularly pleasant night with Stan Collymore recently,
when sharing the pundit's chair down at Talksport – you'd
think their budget would have stretched to a chair each!
– and I soon got to know Stan's demons, and found them
quite congenial and in many ways misunderstood. And as
for Stan? He was like the twin brother I'd never had, and
we hit it off immediately – like a semi-detached house on
fire. Two misunderstood wanderers cast adrift in the
modern game, two drifters off to see the world, two silly
****h***s off for a curry and a couple of lager-tops.
Marvellous! What a night! I was Charlie Big Potatoes!

Exchanging anecdotes, swapping stories, as the night
wore on we swapped shirts, and having run out of ideas,
we decided to swap demons! And so, doing up as many
buttons as I could, I sloped off home in the company of
Sloth and Ignorance, leaving Stan to try to gain admission
to the local flesh-pots with Cant, Bumptiousness and that

---

* Witl*ss.

little fellow from Fantasy Island. Marvellous!

Ho ho! but that was then, and er, this is then too, but er, a bit later on. But I knew it was time for me to make some changes. If Bob Nudge could do it – Ron could do it. I was going to put my house in order!

I counted my blessings and for once I was at one with myself. I felt twice a man! Joan was beside herself – 'three times a lady', isn't it? Bloomin' mind-boggling! How many people were there in my world? And completely miscal-culating the level of occupancy, I ordered a complete back extension to Manager Towers before taking to my bed for three days with brain-fever.

But, be fair, a glimpse into the void makes you stop and take stock! As Joan settled down to a night's television, I made my excuses, and headed out to the potting shed with Bob's gift – *Addicted*, isn't it? Marvellous!

Ho ho! And what a read! Un-put-bloomin'downable. From the very first page, I was hooked. That very night I resolved I would confront my demons head-on. Ho ho! Ron's off the pop! Marvellous, isn't it? And I decided to keep a diary detailing my long journey back from the abyss. Maybe I could get a book out of it myself! And the minute I put pen to paper, it was as if I'd thrown off my ball and chain! – 'loosened my load'*.

Look out for it in your stocking at Christmas. Packed with insight! Untouched by hindsight! And if you're ex-pecting a bodice-ripper, forget it, that's Joan's territory –

---

* In the manner of seventies soft-rockers The Eagles as they was runnin' down the road.

'The rough farm hand took the milkmaid roughly from behind, to the cries of 'Tally-ho!' from the goggle-eyed, in-bred rustics . . .' Ho ho! Marvellous!

Ron, you've been in my drawer.

Er, yes. As I embarked on my new life, I resolved to help those other poor souls who lacked the moral fibre I had been blessed with – 'bottle' if you like! And so, fired with enthusiasm after my first AA meeting, I spent Sunday con-verting the potting shed into Ron's Pop-In. And – blow me! – just as I'm banging up the sign I had my first vis-itor. It's Harvey, from my AA group.

We exchanged cordial greetings and I invited him in.

'Hello, I'm Ron . . . er, I'm an alcoholic, er . . . mar-vellous!'

And immediately we're engaged in fierce intellectual debate. There's more to life than football you know! Don't worry, I'm only joking, it's just part of my recovery. It's one of the twelve steps, 'You must acknowledge the higher power.' And I don't mean the wife – I mean a spiritual power, hmm? And after some humming and hawing over which higher power to acknowledge, we've ditched Sepp Blatter, and plumped for Bacchus, isn't it? And – blow me! – sud-denly, as if out of the ether*, two bottles of Concorde, my favourite blend of British sparkling wine, have appeared on the trestle table in front of us. Should we? hmm? Why not?

---

* US taxidermy lads always have a bottle on hand – keeps the work coming in, hmm?

He was an agreeable if somewhat furry fellow, Harvey, and how we rabbited! Actually, come to think of it, he even looked a bit like a bloomin' rabbit! And he could drink like a fish! But just as I was just opening a third bottle, I've turned round, and – blow me! – he's gone!

So I had to polish it off myself. 'Bottoms up!' – a cheeky little thing with a slight aroma of liniment and athlete's foot – er, the wine, not Harvey! – well, both of them actually. Marvellous!

We ended up spending many a congenial night down at Ron's Pop-In, just myself and Harvey, putting the world to rights. Ho ho! That little button nose, hmm? Er . . .

Nights of frank discussion, tempered with humility at our return from the brink of the abyss, all over a few bottles of Concorde – we never forget the twelve steps, isn't it? However, making my way indoors one night, I lost count, and only got to eleven before stoving my head off the back door. Luckily, I don't think Mrs Manager noticed – though when heading for my Pop-In the next evening, I couldn't help but notice that she had razed it to the ground. Well blow me! Still, every day's my quarter-final, er, second leg these days. Bottoms up! Isn't it? Marvellous!

CHAPTER TWENTY-THREE

YOU ARE WHAT YOU EAT – LITERALLY!

Ho ho! Paaarp! Marvellous!

RON Manager, ahead of his time? Ho ho! The jury's still out on that one! But I always believed a footballer's diet to be of paramount importance. You are what you eat, hmm? Well, obviously you're not, it's a figure of speech for heaven's sake! Imagine a crowd of 50,000 turning out to watch a motley bunch of Pot Noodles and chicken vindaloos tussling ferociously for ninety minutes with a doner kebab and some Heinz Beanz and baconburgers! Ho ho. Intriguing image, isn't it?

Ron, it's just stupid.

Er . . . what's all this sports nourishment about? hmm? What was wrong with good old-fashioned English grub? We're talking about professional sportsmen for heaven's sake – men who need something substantial in their bellies. You can't run a Rolls Royce on, er, rubbishy petrol!

Remember Kevin Keegan accepting the England job? Steaming out of Lancaster Gate and declaring to the press, 'Sausages are back on the menu!'

Ho ho! He nearly got himself bowled over in the rush for the canteen! Mind you, he managed to cause a similar stampede with his widely misunderstood remarks that there was 'plenty of talent in the dressing room'.

Horses for courses, isn't it? Well it would be if your Houlliers and Tiganas had their way. Those Frenchies will eat anything, hmm?

Continental diet? 'Filthy foreign muck' we used to call it! But it looks like the table's turning full circle. Remember Alf Tupper, hmm? 'The Tough of the Track' wasn't it? bolting down a fish supper on the way to a race, hmm? That was the stuff! No wonder Johnny Foreigner's a little apprehensive as he glumly nibbles at his pasta, in the forlorn hope of it helping him withstand the rigours of the Premiership.

Ravanelli! Carbonari! – your traditional bone-crunching English defender would eat them for breakfast. Ho ho! only joking. Not if they could get their hands on a good old fry-up! Chips, bangers, beans, bubble and a slice, all washed down with a bottle of dandelion and burdock – bloomin' powerful stuff! Well, we all knew what dandelion did for you, but burdock? What was that then*, eh?

★ A coarse weedy Eurasian plant having large heart-shaped leaves, tiny purple flowers surrounded by hooked bristles and burlike fruits. Reminiscent of, er . . . cream soda without the foaming agent.

But how many times do you have to plug your ears, rather than have them bent by some nutriti**ist banging on about how the modern approach to fitness and diet has transformed the game? Why do you young 'uns always think you invented it? Take a look at some tips from Ron's Training Manual, *A Good Kicking!* – first published in the seventies but soon to be re-issued in time for the Christmas market. Have Monsieurs Wenger and Tigana perhaps 'borrowed' a few ideas, hmm? Here we go!

1) Stretching: Both arms simultaneously – break wind – cautiously if it's the day after a game – then off for a wee!

2) Nutrition: I've always been fussy about my diet – ask Mrs Manager! A number five egg with three quarter-inch soldiers, or the plate goes up the wall before you can say 'Walter Winterbottom'!

3) Alcohol: The demon drink and the professional footballer don't mix! Well, obviously they do, but before a big game? Light and bitter's your man!

4) Bovril or Marmite?: Ho ho! Isn't it? The jury's still out!

5) Pasta: It's not just for women! Alphabetti Spaghetti, ravioli, macaroni (Ho ho, it's the Chelsea back four, isn't it?).

6) Fish: Hmm? In moderation perhaps, but fishy fish? No thanks pal!

7) Rehydrating: Always drink plenty of water, and pass it frequently and ostentatiously! Ho ho! Great stuff!

8) Bubble & squeak – Er, one of my nicknames actually, when tinkering with your diet, there's bound to be a few side-effects hmm?

Joan, take this one out.

Yet it's all gone full circle now, hasn't it? Many of the fancy Dans from the Continent have woken up to the fact that you can't play a full season in the blood and thunder of the traditional English game without filling your belly with the 'right stuff'.

Take Patrick Vieira – no shrinking violet, is he? Well you don't sustain that level of controlled aggression on a pungent but meagre diet of snails and songbirds!

When he was coming in for a lot of stick over his disciplinary record, Mrs Manager took pity on the poor lad and invited him and Arsène round for dinner. You couldn't meet a nicer fellow! And as a victim of Arsène Wenger's dietary regime, you'd expect him to be a fussy eater. But oh no! Good old English fry-up – chips, bangers, beans, bubble and a slice! While Arsène's glumly pushing a bit of black pudding round his plate, Patrick's wolfed down the lot! And throughout the meal he was absolutely charm personified – ask Joan! Hardly the aggressive, er, 'nutter' painted by the popular press. He even helped with the washing up! Although when I inadvertently got the handle of the chip-pan stuck up his shirt sleeve – Boof! – it's all gone off big-time! Completely out of the blue, he's elbowed me three times in the face – Bloomin' Arsène never saw a thing!

But if, like me, you think the game nowadays has lost much of the languid finesse of its golden years, the modern diet must take much of the blame. When you turned up with your flat cap and rattle to enjoy a feast of football, you knew that a good bellyful of proper English stodge would keep the speed down. You could bloomin' well watch the game without wearing yourself out. As your lumbering defender gathered the ball, you knew you had time to take a munch of your pie, while he steadied himself before lumping it up the pitch to his bustling centre-forward. And should it accidentally bobble to a creative midfielder, the fellow found himself with more time on the ball, hmm? – time to flourish! without any of that haring around like the blue-arsed flies of today's Premiership. And much as I dislike to bring this up – this is a football book! – but is Ron the only person to suspect the presence of illegal substances in the modern game, hmm?

'Dietary supplements'? hmm? Guff! They're all on bloomin' drugs! All that Creatine stuff – we're carnivores, not bloomin' powder-eaters! Why do players today need performance enhancers, hmm? Why do they have to make Viagra so big? Takes just that little edge off a spot of romantic tussling when you have to stop and bolt down a whopping great blue pill – and they're damn difficult to swallow without a couple of tins of that isotonic drink you've probably seen me advertising on cable TV.

Here's a rough guide to a few of the illegal substances that, er, 'awash' the modern game.

EPO: 'Mr Blue Skies', wasn't it? They can detect it by analysing a single strand of hair! If they can detect a single strand among the 'hairdos' of today's shaven-headed, er, 'weirdos', they're better men than me!

Nandrolone: Eh? Won the Grand National in '72, didn't it? marvellous!

Ketamine: Apparently it's a horse tranquilliser! As Big Norm says, 'Just say neigh!'

Kelp: Ho ho! Er, I'm not sure about this one, how does Gordon Strachan keep it up? Easy – seaweed and bananas! – er, Stotin'!

Be fair, some sports have always been full of junkies, speed-freaks and pill-popping potheads. Take the Tour de France, isn't it? Young men in Lycra shorts, hmm? The scent of mimosa – shaven legs smothered in baby oil – out of the saddle – legs pumping like pistons – high on drugs! – saddle sores! er, urinating freely by the side of the road – marvellous! – bit of a bi-cyclist myself actually – I rode a couple of stages of the Milk Race once in the company of a wiry little Belgian fellow. One minute I was flying along at the front of the pack, the next I was dying a thousand deaths – low bloomin' blood sugar! – wasn't it? – And they called it the 'bonk'! – no, really! – Willy to the rescue!

Come off it, Ron.

It was his name, Joan.

'*Want a cocktail, Ron?*'
  '*Ho ho! Don't mind if I do, Willy!*'
  'Belgian mix' he called it! – a 'livener'! – heaven only knows what was in it!* – But I was immediately aware of

---

* Heroin, amphetamines, cocaine, burdock, caffeine, steroids, cortisone and flavourings – marvellous!

a strange vigour coursing through my body like a hurricane! It nearly blew my head off! – Mind you, after a couple of days living on a diet of bananas and muesli bars, it nearly blew my bloomin' shorts off as well! – marvellous! – but it's all a far cry from the modern professional sport we know today, isn't it?

But drugs, hmm? – not a football thing in my day! – A few pep-pills, a couple of jugs of warm ale, and I was 'Charlie Big Potatoes!' – But be fair, the temptation was always there! Once on the way to a charity function, in those heady days when 'El Tel' was weaving his magic down at Portsmouth – me and Big Norm were offered some hemp by a couple of navy lads – *Ho ho! . . . we weren't born yesterday*.

'. . . hemp? . . . money for old rope! . . . No thanks, sailor!'

– On to 'El Tel's', for a wild night, a few drinks and come closing time, a couple of pints of draught ale to take back to our digs – the bar staff most obliging, but no-one can find a stopper for the jug – Well, I wasn't having it slopping all over my trousers on the back of Norm's Vespa, so I've cornered Terry just as he's sloping off with the night's takings.

– 'Any chance of a bung, Tel?' – at which point, I was turfed out most unceremoniously by a couple of big burly fellows in black suits. What was that all about? hmm? –It's a rum old world, isn't it? And so, me and Big Norm spent

---

★ Wednesday.

the rest of the night glumly sharing a huge hubbly-bubbly pipe stuffed with what we later learned to be a couple of fiendishly manipulated Oxo cubes. Marvellous!

CHAPTER TWENTY-FOUR

RON'S DREAM TEAM

'. . . Denis Law, Bobby Charlton, George Best, Alex Stepney. How about you, Ron?'

'Er . . . Mickey Nip, Sol Pardew, Eddie Cleak, Chris Pipe, Bob Nudge, Cliff Richards, Terry Pop . . .'

HO HO! The greatest team of all time, isn't it? Us pundits, we'll argue till we're blue in the face – literally! It's The Top TV Footie Pundit's Annual Charity Fund-Raising Barbecue or 'TTTFPACFRB' as we call it, and we're in for an evening of heated discussion, furious debate, robust opinions – all complete and heartfelt bollocks – marvellous!

Us top TV personalities, we love a good old get-together. I'm a git for a good old get-together!

What? A bit strong? Right ho – what about a bugger for a big old booze up? No?

Me and Big Norm, we're the bonny boys for a big old barbecue* – bangers and burgers – burnt to buggery – the way nature intended! – perhaps a bit of carrot and an onion on a stick for the ladies and vegetarians – ho ho! they might as well get stuck in, it's going to be a long night! When us connoisseurs of the beautiful game are sitting round chewing the fat, you can't get a word in edgeways! And we're not talking flower-arranging! hmm?

What a turn-out! What an assembly of the great and good of the football world – and what a spread! Big Ron Atkinson getting stuck right in, talking about the good old days between mouthfuls of burger.

Just goes to show you, doesn't it? When you think 'Big Ron' you think microwave lasagne, avocado pears, *haute cuisine*! A stickler for it, you'd think. But, like myself, he hankers after the good old days when you went to a football match for the football – a meat pie and a pee at the back of the stand. Marvellous! And he's not that big, actually! The marvellous football family, letting our hair down. Marvellous!

Fabien Barthez! Gauloise and a lady on every arm. How does he do it? He's not that big either. Ho ho! Those fiery Frenchies! A fag 'n' a bird – great stuff! – but to be serious it must be expensive.

Wouldn't it be marvellous if we could all live how we want – defy convention! Cast off our clothes, eat nuts and

---

* Fuck*ers for a free fry-up – heh heh, don't tell Joan.

194

throw caution to the wind! We've all got a bit of the caveman in us, hmm? . . .Where was I? Er, yes!

There's old Fabien coming over all philosophical with a bit of lettuce stuck on his chin. I never knew his girlfriend Linda was a top super-model! – did you?

Yes, Ron.

The ladies love a little baldy fellow with a fag on, hmm?

And don't listen to all the guff – those girls can put it away! If you're not careful they'll steal it off your bloomin' plate – I turned my back to burp, and in two seconds, I'd lost the contents of my hot dog! Linda Evangelista grabbed my sausage, fumbled it between her fingers, stood on it and walked off with it stuck to the sole of her shoe. Not many men can say that! Marvellous!

You see us pundit chappies on television, all erudite and suave, explaining the game to the hoi polloi* with effortless charm, but we can let our hair down like everyone else. Glenn and Chris howling out 'Diamond Lighth' – ho ho – that's Glenn Roeder and Chris Eubank! If you're looking for the real McCoy, Hoddle and Waddle are murdering 'I'm only a poor little sparrow', over by the wheelie-bin as Eileen Drewery stands to one side 'working her magic'.

The big and the beautiful – Sam Allardyce! Utterly oblivious to Ulrika Jonsson cheekily pinching his behind – that's

---

* You lot.

Big Sam! – the Trotters' head honcho! 'Gimme a pig's foot and a bottle of beer!', isn't it? Reminiscent of Bessie Smith in her pomp! 'I want a hot dog for my roll', hmm? Me too, Sam! The night's swinging! And then, blow me, Ulrika's enquired – in all innocence –

'So, what do you think it is that makes a great team?'

And all bloomin' hell breaks loose! Off we all go!

'A great team is always greater than the sum of its parts!' Everything is! It's not rocket science, is it? hmm?

'A great team never says "Die".'

Ho ho! Remember Ron's 'Battling Bone-heads'? The thought of taking a walloping never entered their minds! – Nothing ever entered their minds actually – and if anything ever had, it would have found nothing there to greet it. But those lads never knew when they were beaten – celebrating every crushing defeat with the same vigorous self-abandon as each undeserved point. Ho ho! Blissful ignorance, isn't it? Marvellous!

A slight lull in the conversation, and Ulrika's piped up again!

'So, who would you chaps pick for your all-time greatest team?'

And off we all go again – once we start we never stop!

Big Norm's got Jimmy Hill pinned in the corner, and started barking out his 'dream team' in his usual intimidating manner, 'Batty – Shirtliff – Sheepshanks – Bumstead – Windass – Butt – Dicks – Dabizas – Any queries, Big Chin?' – Ho ho! Jimmy's lost for words – so I've stepped in: 'The Offside Brothers – Noel and Liam, Sol Pardew, Bob Nudge . . .'

Us football folk love a good old a chin-wag. But not with Jimmy Hill, we don't! As he nodded his head in vigorous agreement, he knocked me clean under the trestle table – and I staggered to my feet only to find myself gazing Alan Hansen straight in the eye.

I was immediately entranced. There's something about those eyes, isn't there? Especially in the moonlight. They make you come over all peculiar. What colour are they? I can't tell. Are they blue? They remind me of Liz Taylor or someone, hmm? Or Deborah Kerr, wasn't it? *From Here to Eternity* – Burt Lancaster rolling in the surf! In his pomp! Marvellous.

What a night! Even when the beer ran out the wine was flowing like, er . . . wine does. As the evening wore on we got to arm wrestling, and it's not just brute strength, you know. I'm a bit of a dab hand at it, in fact. Soon I was facing Big Ron Atkinson across the table in the final.

Manager against manager. Big Ron against Ron.

And he soon had that sickly look as I pressed the advantage. Ha ha . . . got him! When suddenly I heard that familiar urbane Scots drawl – I looked round, and it was bloomin' Hansen again!

And with one gaze from his steely blue eyes . . .

I think they're lavender, Ron.

– er, one gaze from those lavender eyes and I was suddenly transported to a sun-kissed beach – tussling in the sand with Burt Lancaster, the surf lapping up the leg of

197

my trunks . . . and – 'WHUMP!'– the full weight of three gold sovereigns, bejewelled identity bracelet heavily embossed with the letters BIGRON and five powerful digits slammed my arm to the table . . . marvellous!

Well, there you have it. I hope you've enjoyed the dizzy ride through the giddy hurly-burly world of my football career and the topsy-turvy world of the managerial merry-go-round – I certainly have. Sadly the time has come to unfasten our seatbelts. A big 'thank you' to everyone for listening, and especially to Joan for her tireless efforts at deciphering my sometimes tiresome indecipherable ramblings. Ho ho! Only joking – false modesty. And be fair, after earning the ultimate accolade in 'punditry' – 'The Pundit's Pundit' – three years running, you might expect me to be content whiling away my time with my wife Joan, walking our five dachshunds on the beach – (that's me, not Joan – I'd be walking them – well not all of them actually, maybe I'd take three and Joan would hold on to two of them, and we'd swap over if either of us got tired), er, yes – home to nights in front of the log fire, Duke, our favourite dachshund, curled lolling at our feet – sounds idyllic, hmm? Enduring image, isn't it? But hang up my boots?

Ho ho! Look out for *Ron Manager: The Next Ten Years* – there's a few chapters yet to be written in the Ron Manager story!

I still have things left to prove, goals yet to achieve. I've said it before and I'll say it again – I may be in the twilight of my career but I always was, and I hope I always will be! There's life in the old dog yet! – ask the wife! Be fair, no point in asking the dog! Marvellous!

Ron, you're not going to like this – it's not long enough. We're going to need another chapter.

Eh? Aw bloomin' heck!

CHAPTER TWENTY-FIVE

RON'S 'DOS AND DON'TS' FOR A MODEL PRO

'Ho! Mr Manager, what do you need to be top plo footballer?'

'Ho ho! Easy, son! Good lungs, a flat surface and two good-quality straws!'

WHO'D have imagined that an untutored lad from Ponders Oak would find himself coaching abroad at Gamba Osaka and Grampus 8? Football's a universal language, isn't it? Hmm? And I'm sure that with 'Mr Lon's' advice, that young lad will soon make his mark – 'as token Oliental in major Plemiership team' – marvellous!

Football's massive in Japan! Well, compared to the size of the players, I suppose. But will their traditional lack of stature prevent them from ever being a world force in the game, hmm?

In the end, it's down to the players, isn't it? Despite my

lack of physical presence, I knew how to throw my weight around! literally!

And who knows what the next generation will throw up? Despite both myself and Mrs Manager being below average height, our son Ferenc grew into a strapping lad with a physique uncannily similar to Big Ron Atkinson – and with the same baby-blue eyes! Marvellous!

Blood's thicker than water, hmm? Well, everything's thicker than water, isn't it? Except maybe wind. In the end it's down to the same old thing – dedication to the old pig's bladder. As a young 'un I was never without a ball, whether it was a trip down to the shops or off to school, I had one glued to my feet – as I weaved through the crowded midfield and the packed defences of my mind.

And I'm still the same! Sometimes I even take one to bed with me – doesn't go down too well with Joan!

In my playing days she'd complain constantly of my dribbling my way to the smallest room, every time I answered a call of nature in the night. Even recently I heard her complaining to one of her beetle-drive cronies about another disturbed night thanks to the old pig's bladder. But you can overcome any physical failings through dedication and sheer bloody-mindedness . . .

Ron, this is all b*llocks. Do your recipes and that.

OK.

CHAPTER TWENTY-SIX

HANGING UP MY BOOTS – PICKING UP MY PANS!

'Football fans have short memories . . . Er, where was I? Ho ho! Only joking! Er . . . No, sorry, actually now I have forgotten . . .'

BE fair, it's the ageing process, isn't it? There comes a time when we all have to reluctantly hang up our boots and call it quits – but don't expect to see Ron Manager shuffling round the bloomin' public library mumbling, 'I used to be Charlie Big Potatoes.'

Don't get me wrong, mentally I'm still that callow youth who blankly bestrode the football world like a nutmegged colossus! But let's admit it, time waits for no man, hmm? As the years go by, and the old bones begin to creak, listen to your body! I do! Swings and roundabouts, isn't it? Your hearing might become worse, but your body gets louder. Ask Joan!

Ron, have you dropped one?

er – ask your dad then! I know what he'll say!

'Ehhh? WHAT?' – ho ho! he's probably deaf as a post!

And, be fair, you've got to let the young 'uns have their chance to sip from the poisoned chalice*. But a word of advice –

When the time comes to leave the dugout, be prepared!

When I finally had the managerial hot seat pulled from under me, I knew I had something to fall back on – in a sentence, punditry!

Ron 'sore-arse' Manager – the devil's advocate. Ho ho! I had 'em on the edge of the seat! Er, not the viewers, er, you know, when the chair was pulled from under me, the, er . . . bovrils had taken a bit of a bang as well.

But as a top TV personality, comfortable in the glare of the spotlight – once you've tasted it, you know, er, you're stuck with it – a bit like kippers, I suppose. If you've got it, you've got it. What is it? I have absolutely no idea.

Personality, Ron.

Yes! Bang on! It's personality! As a player, people used to say I was worth the price of admission alone – and it was two and six to stand on the terraces in those days! From an early age I craved the spotlight! Was I born to embrace it? – not much! From youth, I was the consummate enter-

---

★ Dangerous goblet.

tainer! Playing to the gallery! A couple of song and dance numbers with ukelele! Stripping to my underwear to perform a gymnastic fire-eating routine – unwittingly tucking my still-smouldering torch into my elastic, before launching straight into my poetry recital – 'The boy stood on the burning deck his legs were full of blisters . . .' – at which point my pants began to burn and my sister went off in a huff as I completed my performance in her borrowed beckhams with a singed arse and an odd numbness in my bovrils – marvellous!

So don't worry! Having spent so long as a celebrity, I am well aware of the big hole it would make in your life without having your weekly fix of Ron. Don't despair! When I hang up my boots, I'll be picking up my pans! Marvellous! Welcome to Ron and, er, Joan's kitchen!

Like the idea? hmm? Try some of these recipes! But first let me take you on a guided tour of Ron's culinary domain.

When stepping into the kitchen of Manager Towers, visitors are invariably drawn to one thing, over in the corner, leaning against the wall, slightly battered, flat-bottomed, a little rusty, seen a few years' service – it's Joan!

Only joking! It's Ron's top pan! Or as I prefer to think of it, my one-way ticket to culinary delight – a passport to world cuisine – a present from Nolberto Solano! – the pan I mean, not the passport! Ho ho – Nobby, isn't it? The self-effacing, jazz-loving Peruvian – he might blow his trumpet, but he doesn't blow his own trumpet! Ho ho! er . . . He's not bloomin' blowing mine!

I was a bit of a jazz buff myself in my day you know. I can tell my embouchure from my embonpoint! 'The

Man with the Horn' they used to call me, which is quite uncommon for a pianist! I was quite a 'cat' in my day, and I'm not blowing my own trumpet. Ho ho! Couldn't reach, could you? The cat could, I suppose.

But if you want your taste buds tickled, let Ron tickle the bits that other celebrity cooks can't reach! Bloaters from Margate! Frisky Dumplings! Beef *à la Ronde*! Prawns 'as you like 'em'! Swedish tart! – marvellous! Ask Sven!

While Joan's just getting things underway let me explain the Cabbage Soup Diet. It's great stuff once the guts* get used to it. I got the recipe off that big 'Boro player, er – Windass! He gave it to Gazza too – ho ho! – the recipe I mean! Well the soup did as well, really. Marvellous!

'Who ate all the pies?' That was Gazza in his pomp! Wasn't it, hmm? A little nutmeg, a delicate chip – ho ho! I'm getting a bit peckish here – er, slicing through the defence like a knife through butter with the ball glued to his foot like – like a bloomin' pea on a fork! – I'm bloomin' starving!

Yes, *Hanging Up My Boots, Picking Up My Pans* – Expect it to be essential viewing for those of you whose only experience of preparing food consists of Wisey's old 'Fairy Liquid in the jam doughnut' trick. Ruud Gullit got caught out twice before he tried it himself on Ken Bates – hilarious! Before you could say 'two million netto', Ruud and his sexy football were off to Tyneside!

---

* Abdomen – area between thorax and arse.

But I've always been a bit of a dab hand in the kitchen, and I've recently tried to interest my son Ferenc in the role of TV personality chef. Let's face it, he's got absolutely no idea about the beautiful game. Hardest thing in the world to tell your son, isn't it, but one day, while preparing a nice bit of brisket, I took the bull by the horns, and told him, 'Ferenc, it's not for you – it's someone else's *forte*.' That forlorn look – 'What am I going to eat then, Dad?' Ho ho! Sharp as a tack! Wonder if I can get him on the stage? Marvellous! That's my boy! Ferenc – named after the Mighty Magyar actually – Puskas – the galloping Major! Not our Ferenc, who's more your dawdling minor . . . What was so great about Puskas anyway, hmm? So he had one good game in '53? Bah!

Ron, do cricket or something – it's on the telly now!.

Ho ho! Marvellous, isn't it? The thwack of willow on leather, hmm? Merrie England! Warm beer – straight bat! Stiff upper lip? W.G. Grace! Linseed oil – hmm? – splash it all over! – isn't it? Er, the thwack of baseball bat off bubble-perm! – reminiscent of our Kev in his pomp! . . . Ho ho! Young men – smart but casual – 'Hold my sweater old man' – jumpers for sarongs – er – howzat? – marvellous! – er, why's he rubbing his trousers? Ho ho! – he's thrown a little ball at the other fellow! . . . Cripes! – he's hit it with a small plank of wood! – Marvellous! – Ho ho! – one of them's almost broken into a run! . . . Are they wearing pyjamas? . . . Why are that lot all sitting down? Er, how long does this go on for? . . . 'Cucumber sandwich, old boy?' . . . Ho ho! Don't tell Mrs Manager – gives me the wind! Botham! Get out and walk! Mullet to rival Waddle! Land's End to John O'Groats – Beefy Botham! – marvellous! – who're you calling a pom? . . . Oh, hang on, they're off for tea! Load of old bollocks, isn't it? – hang on, I'll do golf instead.

– Ron's in the nineteenth hole – and they've banned his Big Bertha!

Ho ho! It's a club, not a woman! Er, the nineteenth hole I mean – er – maybe bring a couple of irons next time, hmm? Marvellous! The noble game of golf!

Aw bloomin' heck – er, the beautiful game, isn't it? Well can you think of anything more beautiful? I can't! Pelé perhaps – he was a bit of a looker! I had a passionate three-in-the-bed scenario with old Edmundo nos Paraguaos and Maradona for some time – only for Ken Bates to turn up like a bad penny –

Ron, you're making this up!

Don't stop me now Joan, we're nearly there.

Er – only bloomin' joking! Bloomin' heck! Er . . . isn't it? Well it was – wasn't it? Hmm? Er, marvellous, isn't it? – ho ho! – great stuff! – isn't it? – aw hell's teeth – *JOAN* . . . ?

Ron! That's it – 50,004 words! We've done it!

Ho ho! Yessss! Marvellous! Bugger off!

RON'S TOP TIPS

The Daisycutter

Ohh! It's taken a bit of a bobble . . . GOOoooalll!

Ho ho! 'Keep it down, put it away! Er, pick your spot – but don't keep me awake – Mrs Manager! Ho ho! Just one of my 'funnies'! I always managed to squeeze it in the bottom corner! Ho ho! Indefatigable! Is that a word? It is now! Marvellous!

The Short Throw

Keep your hair on, I've not gone mad! Up you step – they're jostling for position – a darting run here – he's grabbed his shirt! 'Ref! Ref!'

Then, just when they're expecting you to loft the big one to the far post, you drop it at the feet of your nearest team-mate. Ho ho! Makes them all look a bit sheepish, doesn't it? Ho ho! . . . 'Foul throw!? Come off it, Ref!'

The Tackle From Behind

A tricky foreigner is shielding the ball, but our plucky defender is experienced enough to know where it is – and simply retrieves it with a perfectly executed scything lunge at the man's legs. Marvellous!

The Defensive Wall

It requires men who will stand firm.

Men who won't flinch. Ho ho! You've got to be a bit mad! Mrs Manager couldn't watch! I remember her bawling from the by-line, 'Ron, yer nuts!'

The Bicycle Kick

A word to the unwary – not everyone's physique naturally lends itself to this. Use a shaving mirror and the wife's compact to check your profile for unforeseen obstacles before attempting it. My old friend Jimmy Hill once left Craven Cottage on a stretcher after knocking himself cold trying to squeeze one in the top corner!

The Chip

Hmm? The great British invention, wasn't it? Not to be confused with the French fry or those big fat things you get at the Hong Kong Garden – raw on the inside, greasy on the outside. No, for me the perfect chip should be fluffy inside yet crisp and golden . . . Er, hang on a minute . . . Yes! Er, you've spotted the goalie off his line. With practice this can be exquisitely executed . . . 'OOOH! Just over the bar!'

The Nutmeg

A ball struck firmly and accurately through a defender's legs will always cause him trouble – and just a bit of embarrassment, hmm? Red cheeks, isn't it? Certainly will have if the ball takes a bit of a bobble off a divot as it passes between his legs!

The Banana Kick

Roberto Carlos! From Rio de Janeiro to the San Siro – benders to a man! Remember Rivelino, Thumbelina . . . Er, actually I popularised it in the fifties. Ask your dad to name one of the first 'benders of the ball'. Pound to a penny he'll say Ron Manager.

The Professional Foul

Might seem cynical, but it's a fact of life. You probably remember this from those evenings of youth – small boys – lamp-posts their only floodlights – your winger strays too far into the gloom with some burly defender – young boys waiting in the goal-mouth for the cross that never came, marvellous. I hope I'm not going to cause a 'furore' but it's all part of the beautiful game, eh? Well it is, isn't it? hmm?

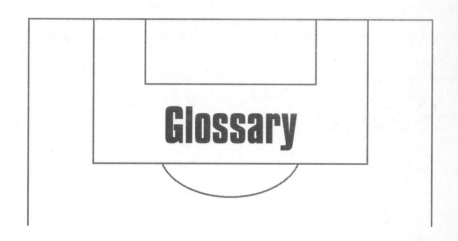

Glossary

Some younger readers may be a little bemused by the mysterious idomatic language used in the world of football – Ho ho! – don't worry! . . . Ron to the rescue! – here we go! . . . this is the stuff you need . . . marvellous!

Aplomb – Er, you know, as in – 'he took that with aplomb!' . . . end of story!

Done his pieces – Easy! . . . he's gone Radio Rental! . . . hmm?

Handbags – Anything from fisticuffs to . . . handbags! . . . I suppose . . . er, Duckie?

In his pomp – Ho ho! . . . isn't it? . . . young men in their prime . . .

Pongid – Any primate of the family: 'pongidae' including gibbons and the great apes.

To be fair – Always deploy before an insult . . . as in – 'to be fair . . . it's not what I'd call a sausage!'

Done up like a kipper – Well just 'done up' . . . isn't it?

Down the gully! . . . Down the gully! . . . – Got me
  beat this one actually . . . next!
Fortuitous – This is just a long word for 'jammy'.
Sexy football – Er . . . not over here mate!
Total Football – Anagram of 'lot of bloat-off'!
Footballing brain – Low IQ – as in – 'he's got a foot-
  balling brain'.